FATHERS & DAUGHTERS

FATHERS & DAUGHTERS

Photographs by Mollie McKool

Text by Bill Porterfield

Taylor Publishing Company
Dallas, Texas

Published by: Taylor Publishing Company
          1550 West Mockingbird Lane
          Dallas, Texas 75235

Special thanks to Southwest Airlines for travel
arrangements.

Library of Congress Cataloging in Publication Data

Porterfield, Bill.
     Fathers and daughters / text by Bill Porterfield:
photographs by Mollie McKool.
          p.   cm.
     ISBN 0-87833-579-X : $14.95
     1. Fathers and daughters. 2. Fathers and
daughters — Pictorial works. I. McKool, Mollie. II.
Title.
HQ756.P67 1988
306.8'742—dc19   87-33679
                                          CIP

Printed in the United States of America

10 9 8 7 6 5 4 3 2 1

To Pops

Whose constant support has always helped me believe in myself and my work.

M.M.

PHOTOGRAPHER'S NOTE

THE REALITY OF THIS BOOK for me began in 1982 as a challenge. Is it possible to photograph a relationship, to capture on film that special bond that exists between men and their daughters? It is a unique partnership, bound by common genes, separated by a generation, and strengthened by opposing sexuality. My attempt to answer that question culminated six years ago in a small photographic study intended for one six-week Father's Day Exhibit. Its popularity kept it traveling for more than three years, being shown in such diverse arenas as art museums and shopping malls. In 1987 it went halfway around the world as our contribution to a cultural art exchange with Australia.

The concept had to be expanded for the book and so I took to the road, photographing fathers and daughters across America. From Oregon to New York to New Mexico to Louisiana to Massachusetts, the response was universal and enthusiastic. Across all cultural and regional boundaries, from the small farms to the large cities, from the man who cleaned fish to the man who performed open-heart surgery, the sentiment was voiced: Fathers and daughters are special...special to each other. Sometimes alike in appearance, in perspective, and in lifestyle, sometimes opposites...but always between the two that special bond.

Allow me to thank a few of the many people who have helped me through this six-year process.

My love and gratitude to my daughter, Kristen, whose special relationship with her father has always been an inspiration to me, and to my son, Eddie, for his love and support.

Special thanks to Jo Stone, John Criswell, Conover Hunt, and Freddie Goff, who all believed from the very beginning when trust was mere interest.

I want to acknowledge Jo Mondo, Beverly Hicks, Sherry Levin, and Peggi Pietsch for traveling with me and for the many hours spent in research and scheduling.

David Rucker hand-processed hundreds of rolls of film and his integrity and skill touched each one.

I will always be grateful to Mark Reedy, whose assistance was invaluable in ways that went far beyond the cameras and the lights, and to David Johnson, whose youthful enthusiasm was always welcome.

My thanks to Bill Porterfield — once an idol, now a friend, and to Peter Larsen, a talented photographer and writer who has always enhanced my images with his encouragement and support.

This book would never have been possible without the openness and sincerity that all the fathers and daughters shared with us. To the memory of Horace Hall and Allison Herrin and to all the others who contributed to this work, who generously let us into their lives and their hearts: We have come away richer, carrying your laughter and your kindness with us.

Mollie McKool

Author's Note

NO BIOGRAPHY, HOWEVER EXTRAORDINARY, can do justice to a single life, however ordinary. So we begin this book of father and daughter images — in photograph and word — with modesty, and something of an apology to those we picture. Primitive people often rebuff photographers. They sense that someone who makes a likeness of them, whether on film or with the age-old doll or effigy, is a shaman who may steal their souls. Anyone who has ever had a painter paint his face and figure, or a writer put him down on paper, knows well the misgivings at the unveiling or turn of the title page. By now we've learned what the primitive knew, that when someone takes your life into his hands, it becomes his life, not yours.

Last spring I had to work up a short talk on the early journalistic career of novelist Elithe Hamilton Kirkland, who sat in the audience as I spoke. With humor, I warned the gathered that in researching Ms. Kirkland's past, I purposely avoided going directly to the source of that experience because I was afraid she would take it back, take it away from me. Because now it was mine, not hers. Being a stealer of souls herself, Ms. Kirkland was greatly amused, and didn't seem to mind the butchery I made of her early years. We pray for the same indulgence of those souls in this book.

But we were direct, not coy, with the fathers and daughters we found, and they have given themselves most generously to us. Some have spoken of their deepest secrets, remembered pain as well as joy, and in some cases I have used the revelations but protected the identities. The stories were more important than the names. But these masked pieces are the exception, not the rule. Every tale, whether naked or a masquerade, is true. Most of the people are who we say they are.

Now, about this soul-snatching business. We make no bones about it. Mollie McKool tried to go straight to the heart of every father and daughter she photographed. As Mollie says, she makes pictures of love, not faces. She sees love one way, I see it another, even when we work on the same subject. It is this combination, sometimes contradictory, sometimes harmonious, that we hope will make these portrayals seem as real and affecting as the people behind them.

We talked with whole families and half-families and atomized families in our search for representative fathers and daughters. By representative, we don't mean stereotypical or normal, because in truth there is no such thing — except by statistical profile, which levels individuals to an abstract mean. Of course, there are families who belong and conform to certain lifestyles dictated by religion, class, wealth, and work, and we've tried to touch upon some of those. But even these supposedly uniform units don't hold up upon close inspection, especially in the give and take of American culture. In spite of the onslaught of mass production, mass communication and pervasive commercialism, somehow we've remained among the earth's most individualistic people, perhaps because of the speed of change in our high-tech world. Yet something deep has not changed, something we share with all the people who have ever lived. Even under the bombardment of advertising and its highly suggestive dream-making, we still listen to the old gods and goddesses of the primordial unconscious. In other words, our souls remember profounder things than 501 jeans, beer with no color or calories, and exclamation-point cars. After all the constants and inconstants of man have spent themselves, the dead-reckoning anchor that pulls him down is the myth of his creation, fall, death, and rebirth; inextricably bound up in that universal genesis is the family, beginning with an androgynous original mother or father who pulls out of herself or himself the mate that will result in sons and daughters to fill up the earth. Hebrew and Christian have only to turn to their bibles to be reminded of the garden. But it is hidden in every cultural expression, even the most blatantly secular and anti-theological. Even so, certainly there is no easy handle on the family of contemporary Western culture, especially not in the psychoplurality of the American Revolution, which continues to this day in the ways that really count, in the groping of highly individual but kindred souls through a cyclone of change. Families try desperately to cling together in the vortex. The successful have come up with some ingenious ways of coping through the maelstrom by creating relationships that defy tradition, or at least shake what we have supposed, perhaps lazily or wistfully, to be traditional. Failing that, family members reach out individually to one another.

"In the 1970s," writes Signe Hammer, a daughter and a feminist, "we discovered our mothers; in the 1980s we are finding our fathers."

In Hammer's 1982 book, *Passionate Attachments*, Ms. Hammer asks why is it so important for daughters to find Father, and vice versa. It is because, she says, the way a woman relates to much of her adult life — which includes the company of many more men in every respect, say, in comparison to her mother or grandmother — is shaped by that "first and most powerful man in her life." Through him, she gets not only her first taste of independence from Mother, but her first rush of love of a man. Little girls idealize their fathers. Young women often lose Father in disappointment, confusion, and even hatred. Today's daughter seeks him out again, looking for the truth, hard and gentle, wishing for the rebirth of a manageable hero-human instead of a marble god, a Satan or a saint, or a Mr. Vanishing Act.

In our pursuit of their spiritual journey toward each other, Mollie and I became something of a family. We loved, fought, split and made up, carried on. And here, in a sense, are the issues of that union, at least all the fathers and daughters. Darwin was right. We are all melted together, no matter what.

Bill Porterfield

A Day In The Park

IT WAS A LOVELY DAY for a walk. As I write this, I smile. Lovely is a word my old man hated when it came out of the mouth of a man, even a boy. I remember once, as a youngster, sitting on the porch with Pa, rocking and savoring sundown. I looked at the red ball dying in the funereal sky and said, "Gosh, Daddy, isn't it a lovely sunset."

He gripped the arms of his rocker and stamped his boots. "Goddammit, boy, ye gonna grow up to be a sissy talkin' that way. Whoever heard of a man saying a sunset, or anything, for that matter, was lovely? Call it purty or something, but *not lovely!* Lord a'mighty, Billy Mack. Where'd ye learn to talk thataway?"

I would bite my lip and steal away like an outcast. I knew good and well that lovely was a perfectly fine word on any tongue, male or female. Anyone could overdo it, of course. That was true of almost any word, especially adjectives. I had noticed that movie stars and theatrical types were wont to do that. They were always kissing one another, even when there was no love lost between them, and saying things like, "That's a lovely, lovely, lovely gown." Shoot, the old man was overreacting. I didn't think I had been silly and simpering. But I shoved that word down, kept it out of manful conversation in that time and that place.

Now I'm free to talk as I please. Now I'm as old as he was then, crotchety and set in my masculinity, much as he was. Stiff hairs grow out of my ears and I walk like a runty grizzly bear. Strange. I see the old man in me all the time. After all those years of running away from him and his hard and fixed attitude, I see he rode my back all the way and that I never really got away. But then again, I did get away, in a lot of ways. And one of them is that I can say lovely until hell freezes over.

So it was a lovely Sunday. It had rained the night before, at least on the Eastside, and now the refreshed lawns and gardens glowed with green in the mild sunlight. It was still a bit muddy, but my daughter Erin and I decided to take her schnauzer for a walk. We strolled over to the fenced playing field at Robert E. Lee Elementary School, unleashed Nobby, and let him frisk about.

Four little Mexican girls, obviously sisters, were playing around the swings, but we didn't pay them much mind until they began screaming. We looked up to see the oldest girl, about eight, running for all she was worth with a dog at her heels. She obviously thought the animal was out to bite her. It was plain to us that the dog was a pup, an awkward and outsized hound, who thought the chase was a game.

In her terror the girl sought me out. I was the only adult in sight. She raced up and fell into my arms, sobbing. I shooed the confused pup away and soothed her. She spoke no English, and I tried to make her understand that the dog was harmless, that it was just playing.

"*El perro no es malo,*" I said.

But as I got the words out of my mouth, more screams came from the swings. One of her sisters, the tiniest, no older than two or three, was fleeing with the dog in pursuit. Somehow she had gotten on the other side of the schoolyard fence and was heading into the street. Matilda is a broad thoroughfare, and with church just out, it was busier than usual on Sundays. One man in a pickup had to screech on the brakes to miss the child and the dog. But he didn't stop and help her. He drove on. More cars came, veering to avoid her.

I picked up my stubby legs and churned toward her. I could have flown to her, I suppose, but too many eyes were watching. Besides, I'm not sure I could have left the ground. My joints have been swollen and painful of late. Still I felt confident of catching her. From the middle of the grounds the metal-mesh fence seemed short enough to leap. As I got closer it loomed higher and higher, but still it didn't worry me. I kept my eye on the girl. She was darting this way and that in the middle of the street. But the time came to consider the fence. Get over it, I told myself, and then get the girl. I guessed it was a good four feet high, maybe almost five feet. No problem, I decided, reminding myself smugly that in high school I had been able to clear a bar higher than my head.

Up, up, and away I went. I felt powerfully light, even heroic. I watched the ground recede, saw the jagged top of the fence sink as I rose. I was almost over. I would swoop down and save the girl. I waved at her and yelled, "*Niña, esta bueno. Yo voy!*"

I did not clear the fence. I plopped on top of it, mangling myself on its sharp points. I struck it with such force that the fence itself, usually inanimate and quiet, rose from its stupor to complain. My daughter said it shook up and down the line as if it would sigh and fall, whining like the strings of an abused fiddle, so powerful was my impact upon it. I hung splayed for an instant until my head cleared. Then I tore myself loose, leaving flesh and blood, and staggered over and swept the girl up from the chaotic street, dancing adroitly, indifferent to my wounds, avoiding flashing wheels and bumpers as did Manolete horns and humps.

As I turned to face her sisters, to reassure them that she was safe, I could not believe my eyes and ears.

They were roaring with laughter. So was my daughter. Even the little girl in my arms began to laugh. Never had they seen anything so funny as my attempts to jump the fence. They shrieked and held their tummies, howling all the way as we walked them home. And as they left us at their yard, I could hear them swarming around their mother at the door, chattering in Spanish, telling her of the funny little man and the fence that brought him down.

"I guess it *was* funny, wasn't it?" I said to my daughter as I limped home.

"Oh, Dad," she said, "you just don't know!"

EARL AND SCAMP

Cordelia. Sir, do you know me?

Lear. You are a spirit, I know; when did you die?

Cordelia. Still, still far wide.

Doctor. He's scare awake; Let him alone awhile.

Lear. Where have I been? Where am I? Fair daylight?
   I am mightily abus'd. I should even die with pity
   To see another thus. I know not what to say.
   I will not swear these are my hands: Let's see;
   I feel this pin prick. Would I were assur'd
   Of my condition.

Cordelia. O, look upon me, sir,
   And hold your hands in benediction o'er me.
   No, sir, you must not kneel.

Lear. Pray do not mock me:
   I am a very foolish fond old man,
   Fourscore and upward, not an hour more or less;
   And, to deal plainly,
   I fear I am not in my perfect mind.
   Methinks I should know you and know this man;
   Yet I am doubtful: for I am mainly ignorant
   What place this is, and all the skill I have
   Remembers not these garments; nor I know not
   Where I did lodge last night. Do not laugh at me;
   For, as I am a man, I think this lady
   To be my child Cordelia.

Cordelia. And so I am, I am.

— *King Lear*, Act 4, Scene 7
Wm. Shakespeare

EARL IS COMING OUT of it now. He's back at the neighborhood bank, and while they're not quite ready to let him make loans again, everybody says it's just a matter of time before he is completely recovered and his old self again.

Scamp, his twelve-year-old daughter, supposes it's for the best, since everyone pitied the new Earl and whispered about his nervous breakdown. The purpose of all those treatments was to get Earl up and at 'em and back in harness, and Scamp realizes that. Still, she found something in the ill Earl — if, indeed, he was sick — that she had never seen in the well Earl, and while she knows he must go back to what he had been before, she hates to lose the new friend she found in him when he was…how did they say it…odd.

His turnabout was such a surprise. The Earl they had known all those years was a forceful figure, certainly a leading citizen. He was a big, lantern-jawed man with huge hands, hands that seemed manfully capable of handling almost any situation, and, sensing this quality in him, they dumped a lot of their problems in his lap.

He was stout on the school board, a Trojan when it came to raising money for the United Way, a pillar of his church. By every measure on the responsibility scale, he weighed in as a solid heavyweight. He was, within the context of his place and time — a small city in Indiana today — a moderately wealthy man, which was even more of a feat when his neighbors considered how poor and ignorant he had been when he first came into their midst.

But it was at the bank where he had shined, as first loan officer. He broke all the rules of lending and made it work for all concerned. All bankers lend money to those who have it, and, of course, Earl did that. But he also rented money to those who didn't have it, trusting in their word in lieu of collateral.

By his own high, hard expectations, he had a way of calling for the best in others. All those homes in the old section that are being bought and restored are the result of Earl's vision as a banker. And yet, he could be hard, ruthless in his exactitude if you did not keep your word with him and make your payments. There were more than a few who could attest to that.

He was a man, and he cut a large swath when he walked about. People paid him respect, rushed to serve him. The waitresses in particular loved him. He tipped handsomely, and was known to buy steaks for the whole house when he was in an expansive mood. The only tacky thing about him was that after downing a heavy meal, he'd pull out a string of dental floss and flick meat from his teeth. If you were eating with him, he'd offer you some floss. He'd insist that you join him in this public display of dental hygiene. It didn't matter if he was in the fanciest restaurant. That was his way and people tried to overlook it. It appeared to be his only flaw.

Well, Scamp herself had a sort of secret complaint about her father. He brought his loan-officer face home to the table and to the lives of Scamp and her mother. He was always in command, though often with reason and affection, and somewhat detached, even in his fond moments. He ran his house the way he ran his department at the bank, like a benign patriarch, and Scamp and her mother were expected to follow his lead, even cheer him on as their champion. Scamp's mother did a good job of it, even when Scamp knew that in her mother's heart was a remnant of the rebelliousness, long suppressed, that Scamp often found rising in her own scrawny breast and beating against her snaggled teeth. There were times when she wanted to fly in the face of her father, but she never dared. She found subtler ways of opposing him, like being more of a tomboy than he thought a proper little lady should be. All of it was a desire to appeal to him, to draw him out of his rigidity and make him recognize her as a pal or even, as she had girlishly dreamed, as a special friend who could care for him in ways even better than her mother. The strange thing was that Scamp got her way with him for a while, almost exactly as she had wished, if not planned.

It began one day when Earl failed to show up at the bank. When he didn't call, his secretary phoned his home and got his wife, who she discovered was beside herself.

"I don't know what's wrong with Earl," Mrs. Earl confessed. "He got up this morning, put on his bathrobe and slippers, kissed Scamp off to school, and instead of coming to the breakfast table, he went out into the back yard and climbed up into Scamp's treehouse. I thought it was a joke, some playful stunt. You know what a tease he can be when you least expect it. But he's been up there for hours and won't come down. He hasn't said a word. It's as if he isn't listening to me. I've never seen him act this way before. I'm in a panic because I want him to come down before Scamp gets home from school and sees him in this state."

It became a crisis. The bank president, even the chairman of the board, came and tried to talk Earl out of the tree. His brother came over from South Bend. The family doctor from downtown. The crowd around the house got so large that they called out the police to disperse it. The word had gotten around, for godsakes, and people were actually driving past to gander. When Scamp got home from school, Earl was still up there. Her freckles paled a bit, but Scamp soon took up a spot at the base of the tree and watched her father carefully, squinting up into the branches with her mouth open. By this time, Earl's brother had shinnied up the tree, only to be kicked in the head with such force that he came down faster than he had gone up. The men began to talk of sending medics up to force Earl into a straightjacket, and that's when Scamp stepped in and took charge of the situation.

"Don't you dare suggest such a thing for my father!" she said in her most adult tone. "Mother, tell everyone to go home. We can handle this ourselves. I want everyone to leave. Holy cow, all he's done is spend the day in the treehouse. I do it all the time." She looked at her uncle and at the chairman of the board and the president. "I mean everyone!"

A silence fell. Scamp's mother broke it by saying in a shaky voice that Scamp was right, that they should retire. She thanked them individually and, gathering strength, herded everyone out of the yard. The brother and the doctor remained, but they retreated to the house.

"Mama," Scamp said, "I know he's hungry. Go fix something and I'll take it up to him."

Her mother looked up into the tree and said gently, "Earl, is it all right if Scamp brings you something to eat?"

And to their surprise, he nodded yes.

He was shy at first and Scamp only got him to nibble a few bites, but when she began to eat with him, he smiled and ate as if famished. She couldn't get him to budge, however. The sun began to set. Mrs. Earl handed up the blankets. It was March and still nippy at night. Scamp would not go to school.

It was three days before Earl, following Scamp's lead, came down from the treehouse.

They took him off to the mental hospital, where, after a series of drug treatments, he seemed to come around a little. At least he was starting to talk with Scamp, albeit in a halting, hesitant way, as if he were a boy again. She was the only one who could get anything out of him. At last they released him, and he came home, a tall, forlorn figure, gaunt now, almost totally dependent on Scamp.

Twice a day she dressed him and took him for walks in the park behind their house. They spent hours playing on the seesaws and swings, chasing the season's new butterflies through the woods and catching minnows in the creek. He would wet his pants like a child. He wept a lot, silently, great tears rolling down his broad face. Scamp never asked why he cried. She just sat beside him, holding his hand.

The love that flowed between them was tender and exquisite, just as Scamp had imagined in her dreams. While Mrs. Earl was grateful for the bond between them, she feared that Earl might remain childlike to the end of his days.

But, of course, he didn't, not the Earl that everyone knew was hiding in the abashed boy. One night, without warning, Earl came down from his room, dressed in a business suit, and walked into the den with such a tread of authority that Mrs. Earl knew, instantly, that he was himself again.

"I'm going to the bank," he said, and bent down and kissed her the way he always had.

"Honey," she said, "it's almost midnight. Johnny Carson is on. The bank's closed. Wait 'til morning."

He laughed. "I guess I'm a little over-anxious."

He was at his desk when the bank opened the next day.

"Thank God," Mrs. Earl said to Scamp. "Everything is going to be as it used to be. Your father is going to be fine and you can go back to school."

Scamp smiled and hugged her mother. But that night she muffled her face in her pillow and cried herself to sleep.

PORK CHOPS AND PROMISES

A QUIET RAIN FELL, refreshing the city. Brick and pavement gave a vaporous sigh and released the blistering heat that inhabited them. Raindrops became little rivers, washing down roofs and gutters and filling drains and ditches. Green grass and blue trees glittered as if showered with sapphire. It was not a frog-strangler, not a gully-washer, but it did wash away the dirt and dog poop and bring the mercury down. This is the way the white side of town saw it.

In the black neighborhoods, especially on the Eastside where there were no proper gutters and drains and sewers, this little rain was one too many. All spring it had come down, flooding the low areas where the poor lived. You could drive out Second Avenue to the Freeway and see the swamps of the river rising to almost road level. Now the muck was green, full of algae, mosquitoes, reptiles, and now and then a body of man or beast, victims of the violence that spilled out of this viney back yard and backwash of the city. In one of the shanties that leaned at the edge of the bottoms, Silverette lived with her father, the yardman, and sometimes with her mother when Mama felt like coming home.

Silverette stood enchanted by the rain. She stood on some rich man's lawn that her father was mowing and let the drops soak into her chubby brown face. She leaned back as far as she could, cheek-to-cheek with the heavens, and took the downpour right on her kisser.

Her father and his mower had taken shelter under the shed of a carport, and he called to her, "Silverette! You come under heah now that you cooled off. And bring the clippuhs with you befo' they rust."

She lingered a moment, then obeyed, dragging the scissors behind her. "Heah," her father said, pulling a rag from his overalls, "let me wipe you off. Now, hand me them clippuhs. They'll rust in a minute and cost like sin." Silverette kept her eyes on the clouds. "Papa," she said, "how long will it rain?"

"Oh," he said, studying the sky, "I reckon thirty minutes or so, or the rest of the day. Clouds fat and bunchy. Look like we'll be coolin' our heels fo' a while. Jus' as well eat."

"Can we eat over there?" she asked, pointing to stone benches under an arbor of vines.

"No," he said, "white folks pay us to keep their yards, not mess 'em up. Come on, we eat in the truck. It won't be so hot now."

They sat in the cab, the windows half-down. The father placed a brown paper sack on the seat between them and, careful not to tear it, opened the bag and began laying out the lunch.

"What are we having?" Silverette asked, all anticipation. They had been at work since early morning.

"Well, we havin' some of those poke chops I smoked las' night. And some white bread and red sauce."

"Pork chops!" Silverette cried. "Pork chops again? We had 'em for supper!"

"Now, Silverette," her father said, "don't give me none o' that whinin' business. You know how you love my poke chops. You ate enough of 'em las' night..."

"Enough to last me for a week," she finished for him.

"Don't get sassy, young lady!"

He gave her one of his down-over-the-spectacles looks that set off the dread in her. Made her feel like she was her Mama, and Silverette didn't like that. She loved her mother, but she didn't like her in the light of her father's eyes.

"They're as good cold as hot," he went on about the pork chops. "I bought a bunch 'cause Sundown had 'em on special, less than a dollah fifty a pound. Heah, put a chop on a slice of that white bread. Soak it in red sauce. Want a slice o' onion? Here. (Silverette rolled her eyes. He gave the same instructions every time they ate chops, and they ate chops at least three times a week. But she let him go on. It was part of the fun of eating, this delight he took in showing her how to savor things.) Eat around the bone, then gnaw on it. Now, Silverette, that's what I call good eatin'!"

"Hmmmm..." she said. "It's good, Papa. And the sauce, hot! More than usual. Got something to drink?"

"Water's all we got. It's in the cooler. Heah, let me help you."

They ate in silence, save for the munching sounds, listening to the rain beat steadily on the truck top.

At last, Silverette spoke. "Papa, when's Mama coming home?"

"I don't know," he said flatly. "I don't know if she will or if she won't. We jus' have to wait and see. It bettah we don't talk about it. If she show up, she show up. That all you can say."

A wind came up and pushed the clouds east. The rain slackened and passed with them. The sun came out in a jubilee of light, drenching the great houses and their spacious lawns in a radiant glow. Silverette took it all in.

"Papa, what part of town is this?"

"Highland Pawk."

"I love it. It's so beautiful."

He nodded, "Come on," he said. "We help keep it that way. And we got to finish. Rain put us behind. If we don't hurry, the grass we cut'll grow under our feet."

She grabbed him by the arm. "Bring me back, Papa. Take me with you as much as you can before school starts. I love being with you like this."

"Then you gotta woik, too, hard as me. You cain't stan' around with yo' eyes bugged out, dreamin' of bein' a rich chile."

"Give me back those clippers," she said, laughing. And she laid into the wet grass, edging it (roughly, then neatly as she warmed) along the sidewalk, earning her way with her father.

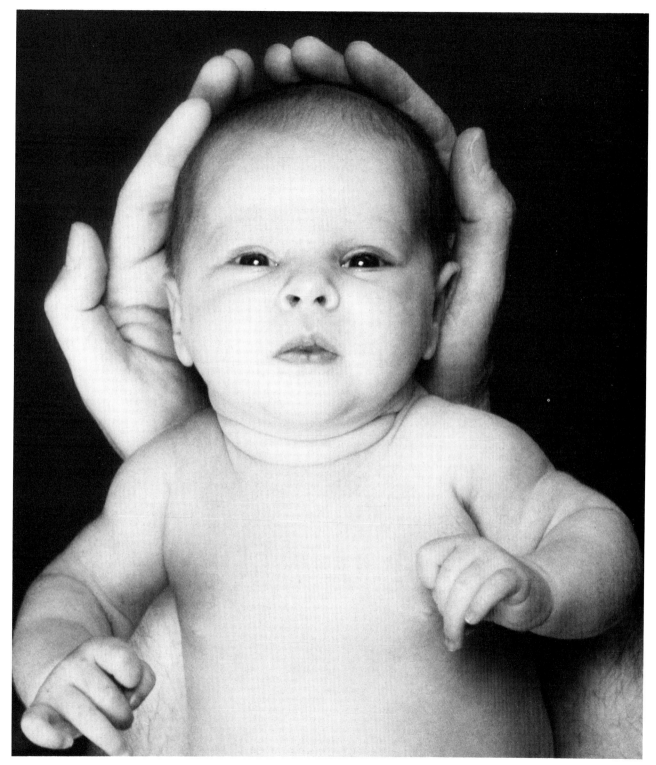

26

Go Girl

ERIN PICKED UP THE BALL of yarn her cat had been playing with and said, "This is my life. Look at it! How will I ever get it untangled? Which string do I pull? It's a ball of confusion. I have so many choices they leave me paralyzed. It's chaos!"

One had only to look around her apartment to agree. She did with her belongings what I do with my eggs every morning. The place was as big a scramble as her head. It mirrored her helter-skelter life.

We are all concerned about Erin at twenty-one. We fear she may crash and burn before she reaches maturity, or, surviving, end up a tough broad, old and used and cynical before her time. It is such a shame, we say, looking at her, listening to her. She is beautiful, with a rollicking wit and a quick tongue. She has the gift to be a wonderful mimic. But she goes at life like a prodigal son, curiously masculine in her self-destructive drive. Her mother prays she will pull out of it. I shake my head and wonder.

I panic at times, too, but when I pause I realize that at her age and stage of resilience she can take a lot of wrong roads and still come out all right. For all the beating she subjects herself to, one gets the impression she is incredibly sturdy. Every day is new, and off she goes. I see in her so much of my own crazy youth that I am cautiously optimistic. This is not to say I am a model of wrong-made-right. Even at this late date I'm still a bit wild and blinky myself. But at least I've leveled out, after all these years, and have taken a path and stayed to it.

The difference between us is one of arc. The swing of Erin's life is broader than mine because she is younger, more energetic, and more adventurous. But her pendulum wobbles and vibrates, threatens at times to lose itself from gravity's hold. My pendulum has steadied over the years because I take a shorter swing. What I have given up in raw power and risk, I have gained in accuracy and consistency. I am happy, at least, to have control of myself, and yet I can't help envying her passion and her reach. She looks back at me, wistfully, and wonders when, and if, she will have my cool economy. I smile and tell her that growing old and practiced is not a trick, that any scrubwoman can do it if she is on her knees long enough. And I tell her that for all the danger in it, I would trade places with her on the gamble that, eventually, I would end up ahead of where I am now as a human being. She likes my saying this, and goes off encouraged.

If she were not such an empty head, I would mean it more. My mind is rich if my circumstance is modest. I suppose I still mean it. I mean it at the time I say it. One thing is certain. I have settled for less than I intended. G.K. Chesterton's remark about Robert Browning comes to mind, mainly because James Kilpatrick quoted it the other day. It is relevant to my purpose as well as Kilpatrick's, so I'll quote it again without qualms. "With him, as with all others," Chesterton said of Browning, "the great paradox and the great definition of life was this: that the ambition narrows as the mind expands."

Once, I saw myself as handsome and heroic, Lancelot. I intended to ride North, South, East, and West, and all the determinants and tournaments in between, so as not to miss a thing. I resented being imprisoned in one little puny body called Billy, and so I wanted to be Mr. Everyman, to see and hear and taste and drink of love and hate and peace and war and everything that life had to offer until I was sated and dizzy with it, and finally wise with it. I tried, but I was not up to it. At some point, I settled into a gear that was not so grinding. My appetite became less robust, my appreciations smaller if not finer.

Now, alas, I am reduced to identifying with some far lesser man. Rumpole will do for me now. Some of you may know him. He is the short, fat toad of a lawyer that Leo McKern plays in the "Mystery" series on PBS. Rumpole is old, Rumpole is ugly, Rumpole is corpulent. Rumpole smokes too many cigars and drinks too much port, and Rumpole's ambitions have narrowed to being a hack for the defense at the Olde Bailey. Ah, but Rumpole is aware. Rumpole knows. He has his limitations and he lets them sing. Rumpole is Rumpole, not a man likely to be copied and reproduced, what with all his flaws. And yet there is something in the warp and woof of Rumpole's astigmatic eye and ironic character that is not only eccentric but universal. He is an original, and, at the same time, he is every little man who ever became old and practiced and crafty. None of us set out to be this way, of course. We aim higher. But short is the fall for most of us. Youth is the great pretender, life the great reducer. To my daughter I say, go girl, and give it all you've got until you are, umm…forty. Then, and only then, need you look back and reconsider.

THE BOND

FOR TWENTY-SIX YEARS, from 1946 through 1972, no politician excited the imagination of the Dallas media more than Mike McKool. What makes this utterly astounding is the fact that McKool lost every campaign he made for public office — there were seven — but one. So what was it about this man that sent reporters, if not voters, thronging to him? Well, we are about to tell, for Mike McKool was, and remains, an American Original, and we are going to be helped in our spinning of his story by his wife, Betty, and his daughter Mollie. Mollie is the gifted artist behind these photographs of fathers and daughters.

In 1968, battling Mike finally became Texas Senator McKool. As the fates would have it, McKool lasted in Austin but one term. As Betty put it, "Mike was the perfect one-termer. He fought for what he believed in as if there was no tomorrow, and there wasn't! Mike was just too much, a great character, caring and capable beyond description. He's sixty-eight now, still practicing law, only he's wooing grandchildren instead of voters. And, of course, when Pops is around, no one else exists for them."

Though limited to one term at the state Capitol, Senator McKool made an indelible mark. In a March 25, 1979 column in the *Dallas Times Herald*, I wrote this about him:

Mike McKool may have been the shortest senator around this side of John Tower, but he was a long, tall talker, immortalized by Guinness as the greatest filibusterer in the history of all the legislatures which have sat since man began keeping records of such goings-on. You may recall that back in 1972, McKool stood in the Texas Senate and talked from 11 a.m., June 26th, to 8 a.m., June 28th — 42 hours and 33 minutes. He sucked three dozen lemon drops, gobbled M & M candy and cough drops, and raised his voice against an appropriation bill that gave short shrift to mental health institutions. For all his verbal virtuosity, the bill passed anyway.

The kicker to it was that McKool was a liberal with a voice as squeaky as chalk on a blackboard. It was horrible to the ears, the worst kind of noise pollution since Rod Stewart sang aboard a Concord. McKool sounded like a chicken that knew you were about to wring its neck, a ruptured duck, a leprechaun with laryngitis, even when he made sense. It was so bad it was beautiful.

It was strange how little we journalists knew of the man behind the dandy on the podium, even though we might leave his rambling house in North Dallas after cigars and cocktails charmed by the brilliance of his personality. There were so many McKool stories that faces got lost in the legend. It was only later that we happened on the fact, for instance, that he was born in Mexico, not of Irish parents but Lebanese, that at Ellis Island his father had arrived as "Mickhoul," a genie instead of a sprite. An immigration official, an Irishman perhaps, *heard* "McKool," and that was that.

This son of non-English-speaking immigrants was graduated valedictorian of his class at Tech High in 1937. College, a war, and nine years later, Mike found himself a senior in law school at Southern Methodist University. One night he went to a Tech Homecoming football game (he had been a last-gasp cheerleader himself, one of the reasons for the raspy voice) where he laid eyes upon Betty Ann Raney, a pretty, blue-eyed brunette sixteen-year-old, ten years his junior. The attraction was mutual. Everyone knew about McKool the war hero, the tailgunner who had been shot down over Yugoslavia and had walked 525 miles to freedom. And most knew he was running for the legislature with this slogan: "Former tailgunner, now gunning for good government." He married the little girl in pigtails on June 19, 1946, and on June 27 came in 2500 votes shy.

"We were so destitute," Betty recalls, "that Sarah Hughes took pity on us and hired Mike to run her campaign for Congress." Hughes lost, too. But ended up as a grand figure of a federal district judge.

"Defeat never belittled Mike," Betty says, not even when the press was constantly referring to him as "the diminutive McKool." He is five-foot-four, which is why he fit so well into the tail of a bomber, but in forty-one years of marriage, she's never heard him mention his stature. "He thinks he's six-foot-six," she says, "and, by God, he is."

He is the patriarch of a maverick but curiously bound bunch. The McKools' first child was Mike Jr., born in 1949, who is now a lawyer on his own, not with his father's firm, and is married to a paralegal. Then came Mollie in 1950, who grew up to marry a lawyer (they later divorced). Matt was born in 1953, and is a lawyer in Dad's firm. Mitzi, the youngest, was born a year after Matt. She taught school, married a lawyer, and has three children. Matt has five kids, Mollie two, and Mike one on the way, and doubtless, they'll all become lawyers or marry them.

So, visiting the clan house, one can understand, as the family expanded, the additions of tennis court and swimming pool, the broader driveway, the child-proof antiques, the toys spilling out of compartments in the den. The McKools are obviously doting grandparents. But how was Mike with Mike Jr., Matt, Mollie, and Mitzi?

"He loved all of them equally," Betty says, "but he was sterner with the boys and disciplined them more. Girls were for smooching and loving and buying presents. Mollie was always Princess to him — that's what he called her. And Mitzi was the Blonde Angel. Mitzi was, compared to Mollie, an angel. She was quiet, a dutiful student, the sweetest, perfect little lady. Naturally, she became an excellent teacher, then she married her lawyer and has the three boys.

"Mike was devoted to Mollie and Mitzi. They could do no wrong. Not even Mollie, and she was a wild hare, the only one without a degree and smarter than all of them put together. She's full of moxie and high jinks, but a bulldozer of resolute, a real composite of Mike and me. She was always in trouble at the Catholic Academy. I think when she finished she had something like fifty detention points against her. Mike was in the Senate then, and when he was home in his study, he would often sign his signature to a pile of blank papers, you know, sort of putting legal nuts away for the winter. Mollie knew where those papers were, and she used them liberally as dispensations from her father to get her off the hook with the nuns. To this day, I don't know if he was in on the deal or not."

And now, from her diary, Mollie McKool on her father:

"If I were to physically describe my father, my description would fall far short of my image of him. To me, he is tall and strong. But the physical has no place, no relevance.

"I've never seen my father cry — not on my wedding day, not at his mother's funeral or at anyone's for that matter. He hates funerals. He sees no use for them. He goes. I've sat next to him at many and he always falls asleep.

"I've seen him laugh, but never uncontrollably. Never has the laughter taken over nor the sadness either. He's always in control of himself.

"But he's not cold. He's warm and caring, only he wants to hide that. He's quiet in his giving. What I respect most about him is that he never keeps score.

"He's bailed so many out of trouble. I've heard his side of phone conversations in the middle of the night, been thanked by strangers for his kindnesses and found out, years later, why they were grateful. If someone comes to him to thank him, he is embarrassed, not a false modesty but true embarrassment. Thank you's are unnecessary.

"Mistakes are handled the same way. An act, a decision is made, and that's it, right or wrong, period. He won't let guilt become a part of anything. Your mistakes are never brought up again. Nor will he allow the people he loves to talk in the past. He becomes very angry with 'what if's.'

"He loves to give things to those he loves. Lots of things — perhaps because he never gave words. He never said 'I love you.' I never really missed it, though I made him say it once. I must have been twenty-five years old, and afterwards it didn't make any difference. People make too much of *saying* I love you.

"I know he loves me. He loves in a way where if you're special to him you know it. He has no patience with most people, no time for things that don't matter. He's always called me Princess and to this day when we talk, if he begins with Princess, I always listen harder to what he's saying because I know it's important. It's something he wants me to remember.

"Somehow he taught me the *bond*. The strand that unites the generations. It goes through us all and if we preserve that bond from father to son to daughter to son, we have within one spirit generations of knowledge and experience. He made it a point that I know his father, even though he died before I was born. I know how he came to this country. I know of his struggle as if I had experienced it myself. And I know even more of my father because I watched his struggle. I guess my dad was, is, the typical American success story.

"Racial and religious discrimination were villains to us. Of the worst kind. Daddy was Lebanese and Catholic, two things Southerners were not tolerant of. Politically he chose to fight those prejudices that he hated. Money and success weren't reasons for his entering politics. He had mastered both of those. Power, maybe, the power to influence people's lives, most definitely! And recognition. I think that's important to him. Being recognized on the street as a friend, a comrade. He likes that.

"In any black precinct in Dallas, he could receive in excess of eighty percent of the vote and more typically ninety to ninety-five percent. He spent a great deal of time campaigning in the black churches. But he never shrank from what he was. Sometimes, he'd take me along. I remember once, he went to a Baptist church. It was dark, darker than any night since. Driving through that part of town, well, the poverty was undeniable. It slapped you in the face and you had to look. I was fifteen, impressionable, and I began to feel ashamed for all that we had, guilty I suppose. And I asked Pops, 'How can you drive here, how can you pull up and step out of a Lincoln Continental? Have you no compassion for these people?'

"I'll never forget what he said. He talked quickly, impatiently, as if at fifteen I should have known what he was going to say, and he was angry: 'Princess, never, never be ashamed of what you are and what you have. Never hide it or change it for anyone. We deserve what we have. We owe no excuses or explanation to anyone. And if you can truly believe that for yourself, then you can believe it just as strongly for others, that they too owe no excuses or explanations. Our political system owes them only *one* thing — the opportunity to attain for themselves.' I never questioned him again.

"Now, my two kids are almost grown, and I think about parenthood. And I remember Dad's old words that night outside that Baptist church. We owe our children one thing — the opportunity to attain for themselves. After that we owe them nothing and they owe us less. After the giving is over it's over. That's love. Anything else is keeping score. I think Pops influenced me in this regard, more than anyone. That's not to say that when family need one another, there's nothing to bring us together. But we come because that's where we *want* to be. It's not guilt or need but love.

"I look at my father as my source. I see his specialness, am tuned into it somehow. His faults, his shortcomings make him human and I accept that. But they are never allowed to overshadow him.

"I see my father in me at times. I hear words come out of my mouth that I've heard from him. I tell my children the same things he told me. The sound of his voice, the rattling of the change in his pockets as he climbed the stairs, echo in me.

"When I began this, the first thing I wrote was that Daddy was tall and strong, at least in my image. But one Christmas some years ago, I believe I saw him for the first time as a stranger would, and he looked small and tired and out of breath, and he was sweating as he went behind the children picking up discarded wrapping paper. Reflexively, I bent over and kissed him. As I stood up, the taste of his perspiration was in my mouth, and I realized in his dear, salty essence that my father was getting old. That taste of him will never leave me.

"I thought of it this last March when Pops had kidney trouble. He was wheeled out of surgery to find five women bending over him with concern on their faces.

"'Do you know who you are sir?' the young doctor said.

"Mike McKool looked straight ahead."

"The question was repeated; still no response.

"I bent lower and spoke loudly into his left ear: 'Daddy, you're gonna have to wake up and talk to us so the doctor will know you're all right.'

"Mike McKool looked straight ahead.

"I knew how to get this stubborn old man to communicate with us. He would never pass up a chance to make us see the humor in life, even at a time like this. So as his straight man, once again I shouted, 'Where'd you hide your money, Pops?'

"Mike McKool did not wiggle an ear nor move an eyelid. Then, all of a sudden, still staring straight ahead, he growled, 'It's in the backyard by the southwest corner under the air conditioner. Dig down about ten feet.'"

"I knew then that no matter what happens to my father from here on out, he is to me — he always will be to me — forty years old, young, with sass and grit and so much left to do."

A FINE AND TRULY AMERICAN BORDER CROSSING

THEY CAME DOWN OFF the Pacific bluff and headed north along Baja California. Anthony geared down the car and purred through Tijuana, then glided into the line of idling vehicles at the San Ysidro border crossing. He smiled at Barbara and winked, patted her hand. "You are beautiful," he said. She was — a golden glow of a girl (1960). Never had they felt so close. Old Anthony (1937) was absolutely lightheaded, playful.

At the booth, the border guard stooped to the car window and gave them the once-over. He was a big, handsome fellow, not much older than Barbara. But his face hardened. Anthony immediately caught it — the thought that soured the guard's disposition. It was the resentment of every young stag who has yet to establish himself and challenge the hoary bucks for reign over the does. Anthony remembered the feeling. It went something like this: Why is life so unfair? Why should all the rich old men who come through here have a pretty young thing on their arm? Anthony was amused. He wasn't all that rich, but he looked it today.

"I suppose you both are going to tell me you're American citizens," the young officer said, fastening his gaze on Barbara. She and Anthony were Appalachian blonds, as pale-eyed as irises.

Anthony pressed his even and very white television-anchor teeth together and pulled his mouth into a grimace. The morning had begun so beautifully. He looked directly at the guard and said, "No, in deference to the other residents of this continent, I usually say 'U.S. citizen.' "

The guard reared back, hand on pistol. "Step out of the car, please," he ordered, "and open your trunk."

Anthony complied.

"Open your suitcases," the guard said.

Anthony complied.

The guard went immediately to Anthony's belongings, flipping shirts and socks up roughly, almost angrily. When he opened Barbara's suitcase, his manner changed. He went through it carefully, respectfully, until he came to her lingerie, which he fingered lightly, suggestively, as if the contraband he sought was Barbara herself, at her most intimate and vulnerable. Anthony watched all this with pure, almost delicious hatred. In another time and place, before men and laws got complicated, Anthony would have already driven a spear into the young highwayman's heart. Now, his only resource was wit and tongue, since he had to answer to the highwayman.

"Where have you been?" the guard said.

"Ensenada."

"For how long?"

"Three days."

"What are you bringing back?"

"Ourselves."

The guard straightened up. "You spent three days in Ensenada and you're not bringing anything back but your selves?"

"That's right."

"Now, let's go over this one more time. You were in Ensenada three days and you claim you didn't buy anything?"

"No, I didn't say we didn't buy anything. I said we aren't bringing anything back."

"What was the purpose of your trip?"

"Just…oh, I don't know. Pleasure. A holiday. Just to spend the weekend."

The guard pulled out a form, wrote on it, and slipped the paper into a magnetized clip and placed it on top of the car. "Drive over to the secondary search area," he said.

Anthony complied.

They sat in the roadster as a second guard approached. He read the note from the first office, looked at Anthony's identification cards and then Barbara's, had a third officer take their driver's licenses into an office to check them out on a computer. "Where have you been?" the second guard asked.

"Ensenada."

"What was the purpose of your trip?"

"That is none of your business."

"What is your relationship to the young lady?"

"And that is none of your business."

"Sir, you are required by law to cooperate with Customs and Immigration when you are returning to the country."

"I'm required by law to make a declaration to Customs, to allow myself and my possessions to be searched, and, if required, to prove my citizenship. I've done these things. I'm not answering any questions about the purpose of my trip or my relationship to the young lady. If you want to ask me about contraband or customs duty or my citizenship, I'll be glad to cooperate."

"We'll see about that. Step out of the car, please, both of you."

Anthony and Barbara complied.

A supervisor in a grander uniform took Anthony into the office. He was an older man, quiet and matter-of-fact. "Why are you refusing to cooperate?" he said. "We are only doing our jobs."

"You're not doing your job when you question me about the purpose of my trip or my relationship to my companion. You people are not morals inspectors. You are customs officers charged with guarding the border, not with checking out the weekend doings of U.S. citizens."

The supervisor went out and got the first guard, the hot youngblood. They conferred. In the meantime, the second guard had meticulously searched the car and their suitcases.

"Sir," the supervisor said, "do you know we can strip your car down, take it apart piece by piece?"

"That's between you and Hertz Rent-A-Car. I don' care what you do with it."

The third officer came up with the driver's licenses and handed them to the supervisor, saying that they were in order. The supervisor grunted, sighed, and handed them to Anthony.

"Mr. Garrett," he said, "you and your wife can go."

Once on the highway to Long Beach, Barbara giggled and punched Anthony on the shoulder.

"Daddy," she said, "it's great to be with you again after all these years. No wonder you drove Mother crazy. You are a *mess*."

He started laughing. She joined him. They roared until they were teary and red-faced.

PERSISTING, PROCREATING

"A DAY LATE and a dollar short" was my father's favorite expression. He applied it first to himself and then, with amazement and chagrin, to my brother and me. There was clearly no breaking of the mold. His mark was upon us. We would always be a day late and a dollar short.

I see it now in my children, and I shudder. How long do these negative hand-me-downs continue? And how does nature cull them? Do we go down with our genetic weaknesses or do we shake them off and triumph? So far, about the best you can say about a Porterfield is that they have survived. And I suppose that is something in itself, given the cut of the caul.

The other day, my friend Laurie said something out of the blue of an airy conversation that I'll not forget. She said of this mutual friend that "he never got to the soft middle." Laurie has a habit of saying things that go to the heart of the matter. It struck me that this friend of whom she spoke must be a blood brother. To test the kinship, I called him and asked if he had filed with the IRS.

"No," he said, "I'm a day..."

"...late and a dollar short," I finished for him.

And yet one persists, even procreates.

By this time tomorrow, I should be a father again, for the first time in twenty years. The sonogram suggested it will be a healthy girl. Certainly she's a kicker. Oren is her name. I have stared over and over at the almost opaque yet quite transparent picture of her the sound waves recorded as she squirmed in her mother's womb.

I fancy she has my round head and her mother's large, dark eyes. The nose looks like it has a slight Lebanese hook in it, which I, with my Irish pug, welcome. Beauty is in the bones, not the flesh, and surely that kind of angular architecture will elevate the line, which on my side of the family has tended toward the round and the squat.

Those who know my history and who creak with me into the far side of middle age think I am daft for "starting all over again." Any experienced parent can recite chapter and verse the pain of mothering and fathering, especially those of us who have lived through the assault of puberty upon our young. There is nothing more selfish or demanding than a child, unless it's an adolescent or a new adult. And they are like cats. They give little in return. Eventually they come around, usually when they themselves are becoming parents, but often it's too late. You're already on the edge of the grave. Thanks a lot, kid, thanks for the funeral flowers.

But still, they are more than worth the sacrifice and grief, in and of themselves. And it's nice for the ego that they carry on some of you and your beloved. One has to agree with Germaine Greer, that barren and beautiful old feminist who now concludes, with surely some rue, that "most of the pleasure in the world is still provided by children" and not by the sterile "genital dabbling" of the childless modern.

They pull you out, children. They make you get up and go with them. They make you see the world anew as they are seeing it. They also pull you in, children. They make you lie down and snuggle with them. They make you feel as wondrous as they are feeling. This isn't sentiment. It's the shrewdness of Mother Nature. She makes the young so cuddly, even hyena and jackal cubs, even tender Porterfields, that parents cannot but coddle and protect them.

I need this at fifty-one. And I will be a better parent than at twenty-eight. I am a better gardener now. There's been little sun this spring and many storms, but my carrots and corn fairly burst through the sod of my tiny urban plot. And now that I've committed myself, strewn my seed after all these years, the genes will have to take care of themselves, just as Oren's half-sister and half-brother take care of themselves as they come, at last, through the rye.

There is, of course, more to a person than genes, and the part of Oren that reaches out to Daddy I will happily care for, as Holden Caulfield did for his sister Phoebe and all children in J.D. Salinger's *The Catcher in the Rye*.

At one point in the novel, Holden says, "I keep picturing all these little kids in this big field of rye . . . If they're running and they don't look where they're going I have to come out from somewhere and catch them. That's all I do all day. I'd just be the catcher in the rye and all. I know it's crazy."

Beautifully, affirmatively crazy.

Hang In There, Dad

EVERYTIME SHE LOOKED UP, he was there, his bright, undeniable face raised in expectation. "I'd come out of class," Susie said, "and he'd be sitting at the bottom steps, waiting. He didn't have much more money than I did, but he'd have a gift. After class, I worked as a clerk at Scarbrough's Department Store, and when I'd come home at nine he'd be there with a record that I had mentioned I wanted."

"I completely let go of all my inhibitions," Paul said. "I was so in love, and having so much fun with it, that it was nothing for me to bike twenty miles and back to see her."

"He was irresistible," Susie said. "His hair was blacker and longer than mine, and he had these great eyes. And he was so handy! He started cooking my dinner, typing my class papers, even reading my textbooks and helping me with my homework. I had never seen a man like him. He was so caring and competent. And if he didn't know how to do something I needed done, like repair my car, he would see that it was done. More and more, the details of my life began to fall into his hands.

"You see, up to Paul, I had an aversion to depending on others. It goes back a long way. My mother, Jolaka, or Jolly as we called her, was Hungarian and she had had a hard life, surviving Auschwitz only to die of cancer when I was eleven. Her death was a loss for me and my sister, but it so devastated my father he had a heart attack and never recovered enough, psychologically, to care for the family. We had to do a lot of growing up by ourselves. As a student I was very much on my own. When I needed money, I earned it. When I got hungry, I cooked. When my car broke down, I saw that it was fixed. And I was sick of doing everything for myself. I would have loved for a man to come along and do it for me. But no one came through until Paul came along."

Susan Katz wanted a husband in the oldest sense of the word, which meant Mr. Fixit and progenitor of children. In the Freudian connotation Susie was seeking the father she felt had been absent in her life.

Paul Nicholas Gold remembers meeting Susie's father at the beginning of their courtship: "Herbert Katz was from a wealthy Jewish family of Berlin. The Nazis had stripped them of everything. He had come to America when he was about forty. His work required him to travel, and he was very knowledgeable. He spoke in a heavy German accent and reminded me of Henry Kissinger. He was extremely intelligent, and I liked him, still do. He's still in the picture."

Susie is more reserved: "My father couldn't be a father, absent as he was both because of his work and because of his grief over the loss of Mother. When he was around, he was Germanic and authoritarian. He was forty-eight when I was born, so you can imagine the situation. Now, as an adult, I can see why Paul enjoys him."

The fact that Paul and Susie were cultural Jews, if not absolutely kosher, helped them in their quest for a traditional family. But let's not get ahead of them.

Throughout their courtship, Paul remained Susie's get-it-done-guy. He was determined to prove his dependability. So he ran himself through a gauntlet of trials, which he imagined were tenpins Susie had set up to test him. Whoever set them up, Paul knocked them down, sometimes with ease and sometimes with difficulty, but he proved himself to be as durable as he was passionate and committed. Susie had obstacles to overcome as well, the main one being her stubborn self, the other his parents — especially Paul's mother — who were not so much against Susie as they were the idea of such an early marriage. Both were nineteen.

They waited fifteen months before they wed. But they did not wait for love, and at one point during their engagement, they sweated out a false signal that Susie was pregnant. In the light of the story that unfolded, this would be looked back upon as a great irony.

One of the big things Susie wanted out of their life was children. Paul wanted a family too, but he hadn't stopped long enough in his rush to be a lawyer to consider what it meant to be a father. Certainly he had no idea how hard it would be to have children. I'm not talking about the difficulty of bringing up children. In the Katz/Gold case, we're talking about the woes of conception.

By 1977, four years into the marriage, Susie knew she had Stein-Levanthal disease, meaning her ovaries were so cyst-ridden it was difficult for them to release eggs during ovulation. This messed up hormones and enzymes and generally upset the balance of her reproductive system. Still, Susie was intent on conceiving, preferably before she was thirty. This was the beginning of what Paul calls The Marathon. At first Susie tried medication, even had a wedge section — the removal of large parts of one ovary and almost all of the other. "A hysterectomy would have been easier," she recalls. "We were settled by then, and I was assistant director of the banking school at the university. I had to take off six weeks because of the operation."

Recovered, she and Paul went at procreation with new heart, but nothing happened. Susie went back on exotic medications, which made her retain water, bloating her.

It was about this time that they started the thing with the charts. Every morning, after exactly six hours of bed rest, Susie would take her basal temperature and note it on a chart, which she and her doctor studied in search of a pattern to her ovulation. The instances were so irregular they couldn't predict when she would ovulate. In a healthy woman, the basal temperature dips two degrees 24 hours before ovulation, then rises quickly by several degrees at ovulation. To conceive, the male sperm must enter the ovum during this pre-ovulatory dip. The faint signals from Susie's ovum made it a difficult target for Paul's army of sperm. She kept at her bedside an extensive chart of temperatures and Xs, which stood for the times they had intercourse. For five years, at home or work, Susie lugged about her thermometer and chart, checking her temperature. And every month, during the five days surrounding ovulation, Paul was on alert. He might be at the law office and she at the university, he might be on the freeway and she at the supermarket. Wherever, she would phone or beep him with the same urgent message: "Meet you at the house as soon as you can get there. THE TIME IS RIGHT!"

Attending a convention in a nearby city, Susie awoke one morning in the Hyatt Hotel, took her temperature, called Paul and had him drive forty miles as fast as he could to do it.

"I lived on the fly, so to speak," Paul says. "My colleagues at the law office and at the courthouse called me SuperPaul, because at a moment's notice I was ready to jump into a telephone booth, disrobe, and leap tall buildings in a single bound to be at my lady's beck and call."

In October of 1978, they learned that SuperPaul's sperm, if ever an army, was a depleted one. His count was so low doctors feared his sperm were not reaching Susie's ovum. So from then on, at ovulating time, they had to stop having bedroom sex and try to unite sperm and egg at the doctor's office. When the charts deemed that the time was nigh, Susie would have Paul meet her at the doctor's. While she waited on her back under the lamps, Paul would take two specimen vials and head for the men's john, where in the cold utilitarian closet he would secrete the precious if weary sap of his genetic covenant into the vials and take them to Susie. She would place them in her bra to keep them warm until the doctors could artificially inseminate the seed of her husband.

One can imagine it was difficult for both of them, devastating to their once-bounding physical relationship. They felt like laboratory mice instead of lovers. When it counted the most, sex took on the chrome and clockwork of the clinical and impersonal, all under the probing eye and instrument of gynecology. The bedroom did not become a retreat from the laboratory, but a psychological extension of it. They knew that Paul's sperm count grew stronger with abstinence, and they felt guilt about wasting sex that would not produce a child. And they needed each other's warmth and passion. Many nights they clung together in silent depression or in tears. And the lower their spirits got, the stingier their bodies became. Paul's sperm count dropped, Susie's ovulation became a trickle. It was a Catch-22.

Yet they persisted, these striving descendants of Abraham, David, and Solomon. Susie had aroused in Paul a desire for children, and now, maturing as a husband and provider, even astonishing himself with his performances in the courtroom (now he was not intent on reforming the system, but rather using it to his client's advantage), Paul was stout as ever in the service of his wife. He had to become a mechanical man to do it, on call to perform under the most stark and chilling circumstances, but he bore up under the indignity and persevered.

It was not enough.

One day the doctor put a proposition to Paul. He had found an intern with a strong sperm count who bore a resemblance to Paul, a man who not only shared the blood and traditions of Abraham, but who shared Paul's place on the curve of intelligence and education. This man would never be known to Paul and Susie, but the doctor could mix his sperm with that of Paul's, and, metaphorically speaking, help this modern Paul on his road to Damascus. If Susie conceived, it might well be Paul's sperm, pushed and encouraged by the donor's. Since there was no easy way of telling which way it went genetically, what difference would it make, as long as a child was conceived to Susie?

Paul simply wasn't ready to concede the fight.

It was during this period that the Golds shrank from suburban friends and withdrew into themselves. All around them, couples were having babies. Some who didn't want babies were having them and complaining. Some were having abortions.

Paul and Susie continued to try to make a baby, but they were becoming physically and emotionally drained, so they pursued a fallback: adoption. They signed up for a newborn at an adoption agency. The application was sixty pages long, and one of the questions that jumped out at them was the matter of psychological counseling. Had either of them been to a shrink? They both felt the need of counseling, indeed, hungered for it, but now they were relieved that they hadn't gotten it because they could write in the blank, "No." They later learned that this was not necessarily a hindrance to adoption. Even after being approved, they had to wait for two years to get on the waiting list.

But, of course, by now we know that Paul Gold would not just sit and wait, a faceless name at the bottom of a slow-moving countdown. When he had searched for work fresh out of law school, he had gotten jobs by sheer endurance and pluck. "I may not be the fastest," he says, "but I had staying power and chutzpah. I got jobs by sitting in the outer office longer than any other applicant, so long that when the boss got up to leave for the day, he'd have to pass me, as he had when he came in that morning, as he had when he broke for lunch at noon." Every chance he got, Paul popped into the adoption agency, tipped his hat and said, "Hi. Paul Gold. I just wanted you to know I've driven forty miles over here to tell you Susie still isn't pregnant and we want a baby. Thank you. Now I will drive the forty miles back home to a house barren of children."

The agency served the Golds in a way neither would have imagined. Once their application was approved, and Paul felt welcome when he dropped by their office, it became simply a matter of time before he and Susie would have their baby. They relaxed for the first time in five years. You can guess the rest.

On March 23, 1981, Susie learned she was pregnant. Three days later, the people at the agency called to say that they had a baby waiting for them. The Golds jumped up and down, but they came to earth prudently. Fearful of a miscarriage, they informed the agency of their situation and asked to be allowed to remain on he list until Susie and child were in the clear. At three months, all signs were go, and the Golds removed their names from the adoption waiting list.

Jordan Lindsay Gold was born December 7, 1981, after a long and arduous labor. She was a dark-eyed, dark-haired girl, a clone, Paul says, of Susie, who was a clone of her mother Jolly, and thus, in memory of the Hungarian Jewess who is a heroine in their eyes, they named the child with a J, after her and the river she had crossed. Indeed, the river they all had crossed.

Jordan has grown into a beautiful girl who has a passionate thing for her father, and well she should. Susie says no man makes over his daughter as does Paul Gold.

Nor she her son. To their astonishment, Susie turned up pregnant again. And on June 30, 1986, to them came a black-eyed boy, Alex, making complete this fine and inspiring contemporary American family of the Katz/Gold line.

As Paul says: "Some fathers want children to perpetuate themselves or their name. I wanted children to multiply and perpetuate the love and joy I found in and with my wife. I can truthfully say, without hesistancy, I have obtained what I was after and think every moment we spent seeking it was worth it."

A Reunion, Of Sorts

WHAT HAPPENED BETWEEN DAVID GATES and his wife Loraine is none of our concern. They themselves would never speak of it. What is important to this story is that some time in 1939, as the war that would ravage half the globe began in Europe, Gates left his wife and two-year-old daughter Laura in Denison and went to sea, never to return. Loraine got a divorce and she and the child simply disappeared, as far as Gates was able to tell, into the vastness of America. Some years later, after he got out of the Navy, Gates tried to find them but could not. In 1947, he married a woman named Nina, and raised a son and daughter.

For years, Gates worked in the old Records Building as a county service officer for veterans. He was a fine-looking gentleman, about six feet tall with a head of white hair and a fatherly manner about him. He walked with a limp from a wound he got in an explosion at sea. He was a steadfast family man, a churchgoer, rather conservative and conventional in his values and lifestyle. And for thirty-eight years he had lived with a nagging guilt about having lost his first daughter Laura.

He would come to find her, but too late. David Gates was never to know what a splendid woman Laura had become until the day of her funeral. The irony of it was that they had lived in the same city, both working and raising a family, without knowing that the other was there. In fact, Laura, a journalist/photographer, was often on assignment in the public building where her father worked.

On Thanksgiving Day, 1977, Gates was at home with his family when a distant relative called by telephone to tell him to please read the morning's paper. It carried a wire service story from Richmond, Virginia, about a small plane crashing at an airport there on Thanksgiving Eve. The plane had carried three passengers, a couple who had taken turns piloting the craft and their sixteen-year-old daughter. The couple was well-known, the noted photographers Bob Smith and Laura Garza. The daughter,

Carla Garza, had walked away from the crash. Bob Smith, the girl's stepfather, was critically injured. His wife, Laura Garza, had been killed. The dead woman, the caller regretfully informed David Gates, was none other than his long-lost daughter.

Gates learned that Laura and her husband and daughter had flown into Richmond to spend the holidays with Laura's mother and stepfather. Years before, Loraine had married a man named Charlie Slade. Charlie had been the only father Laura could remember.

The following Monday, a bereaved group of family and friends gathered at St. Stephen United Methodist Church to remember Laura Garza in a memorial service. It was a cold, wet November day, dark and dreary, but the church was packed. Bob Smith, himself an ordained Methodist minister, lay unconscious in a Richmond hospital. His wife's body, according to her will, had been given to medical science. But Carla Garza was at the church with her brother, Benito, and their father, Carlos Garza, both of whom had flown in from California. The Slades had remained in Richmond at the bedside of Bob Smith. As the mourners settled into the pews, a tall, white-haired man limped quietly into the church and stood at the foyer. A collection of photographs on the wall caught his eye. They were candids and portraits of Laura. For the first time since she had been a child, David Gates laid eyes upon his daughter. He wept.

And he came to have a sense of her as he listened to Patsy Swank's eulogy. Patsy talked of her long association with Laura at Channel 13, of Laura's peerless gift for producing picture essays, of her love of art and music, particularly Picasso, Mozart, and Verdi, of her passion for Latin America and Mexican food, and of her flair for flying.

It was, of course, not enough for David Gates, though that day he left the service for Laura without telling anyone who he was. He decided to be tactful and wait until Laura's survivors had had some time to deal with her death.

Months later, after Bob Smith recovered and returned to Dallas, Gates used a go-between to make himself known and to ask if Bob and Carla (Benito had returned to California) would met him for lunch. They sent word that they would, although they were still heartsick and shaken by the tragedy. Smith particularly had a bad time because he tended to blame himself for the crash. On a Sunday in March he and Carla gathered with the Gates family at the Circle Grill. Gates brought his wife, Nina, and his son, Bill, a twenty-eight-year-old policeman. It was awkward but they got through it. Later, Bob Smith would say that he said to himself, "Yeah, this is Laura's father. She had some of his mannerisms. They lived in two different worlds, but the old gentleman shared her intelligence and sensitivity." And Bob was pleased to see in Bill, the half-brother cop, some of Laura's artistic bent. Bill played the piano and painted.

As for David Gates, he was spellbound by his granddaughter. "She's the most beautiful thing I ever saw," he cried. He said it over and over. He wrote her and her stepfather later:

"I waited as long as I felt I could before imposing this additional burden on you, but after hungering to see Laura for so many years and finding her when it was too late, I was terrified that something would happen before I could see Carla and Benito...I have a great measure of guilt to bear which I am sure is deserved. Nina said I could have tried harder and done more to find Laura. This will add to my burden during whatever time I have left here."

Gates asked for and received photographs of Laura and Carla. "He was voracious," Bob said. "He wanted everything we could find that related to Laura and Carla."

When Carla played a part in her high school's production of *My Fair Lady,* Gates went to every performance of the two-hour play. He showered gifts and attention on Carla, fawned over her to the point that it made her uncomfortable. She wanted to please him as best she could, but she needed more time and distance. Biology was not enough. He was still a stranger to her, and she could not forget what a stranger he had been to her mother.

Laura had, indeed, wondered about her father. Once, while photographing gravestones for a "Spoon River"-like story we were doing on the dead of Garden Valley Cemetery in Van Zandt County, Laura noticed some Gateses were buried there. "That was my father's name," she said pensively. "It seems to me he came from this part of the country. This might be his kin, and mine. I was a baby when he left, and, of course, I never knew him."

"Do you miss him?" I asked.

"Well," she said, brightly now, "you can't miss what you don't remember having, can you?"

"I guess not."

"I do wonder, though Charlie Slade has been a most wonderful father to me. Mother never spoke of my real father, and I have little idea what he was like."

Carla's growing coolness bothered David Gates, and he sensed that he should back off. But October 2 was coming up. Laura's birthday. She would have been forty-one. Gates wanted to see Bob and Carla, but he didn't dare call. It was just as well. On that day, especially, each of them wanted to be alone. But Gates felt he had to talk to someone who had known Laura.

So he got in his car and drove over to Channel 13. He knew that Lee Clark, one of the executives at the station, had been a friend of Laura's. He walked in and introduced himself to Lee as Laura's father. Lee was stunned, and then moved. She talked and helped him as much as she could, and then she sent him to Patsy Swank.

"He was like a dry sponge," Patsy said. "He soaked up everything I could think of to tell him about Laura. It was strange. Here I was trying to explain to a man what his dead daughter had been like. But you know how Laura was. She was so splendid you could talk for hours about her, and Mr. Gates was a passionate listener."

On October 2, he sent flowers to Lee and Patsy. The note said, "Today is Laura's birthday. May I attempt to thank you for your kindness?" Patsy read it and cried.

That was ten years ago.

Carla and her brother Benito have since gone the way of all children and grandchildren. They've flown the coop. After several years working as a waitress and trying to make it as an actress in New York City, Carla moved to California, where she and her boyfriend, Tony Berkerley, opened Little Louie's Deli and Ice Cream Parlor in Point Richmond, a suburb of San Francisco. Carla has remained in touch with David Gates by occasional letter, and in March of 1986 she invited him to her wedding.

Everyone, including Mr. Gates, was there except for Loraine and Charlie Slade. Laura's mother has cancer and is bedridden. Bob Smith was there with his new wife, Linda, and even Laura's first husband, Carlos, father of her children, showed up. He gave Bob a hug and helped set up a videotape show Bob had made of Carla's life. The tape included many photographs of Laura, even one of a young Loraine with a young David Gates. Bob said Mr. Gates must have played the tape and watched it ten times. Then he slipped out into the back yard and remained there. At the edge of things, as if he felt he was an outsider.

Bob went out and asked him to rejoin the party, but Mr. Gates declined. Finally, Tony went out and talked to him, and they returned to the others arm-in-arm. "From then on," Bob said, "Mr. Gates settled in and seemed to enjoy himself."

NEW BEGINNINGS

SPRING AGAIN AND YET still new beginnings. We are blessed by the ongoings of nature, even those of us with scaly bark and ancient sap. I leaf out one more time this April, and return from sabbatical with a two-week-old daughter and a new place in life. How can a man ask for more than renewal? All the Lazaruses are my brothers, the Marys and Marthas our sisters, and we are at home in the heart of the city, singing the life-affirming Beatles song:

You say stop
I say go
You say why
And I say I don't know
I don't know why you say goodbye
I say hello
Hello, hello
I don't know why you say goodbye
I say hello

The new Margot Perot wing of Presbyterian Hospital is like a Hyatt Hotel of maternity. The soaring atrium that greets in the lobby takes you to the roof, and this heady sense of elevation, this mode of light and height and modernity stays with you and your lady, and eventually with your newborn, as you go from labor and delivery, recovery and a room of your own.

Give or take an old grouch or two, the staff was wonderful, particularly Fifth Floor station nurse JoAnn Thompson and Helen Hiatt, the breastfeeding instructor. Thompson and Hiatt are mothers as well as registered nurses, and their way with patients was rich to behold. Here came Thompson, full-bodied and quiet, a gentle Mother Earth, and after her Hiatt, a tiny, intense Fairy Queen waving her wand over mammary and milk. Everything came off as scheduled, this union of nature and medical science, and I, a veteran father, left the hospital feeling that paternity was not an abstraction after all. No pacing the lounge and halls awaiting word. I had been in on everything from start to finish. They even let me hold Nanette's hand in the delivery room. When Oren was pulled from the womb, they handed her to me, and I presented her to mother. Nanette, thanks to an epidural, remained alert and gabby throughout the Caesarean.

The manner of them that did the cutting and stapling of Nanette's tummy was an amusing surprise. Dr. Laura Gambini Blocker was our obstetrician, assisted in the surgery by Dr. Eugene Hunt, III. The way I see it, the lady doc's got the world on a string. She's a fetching strawberry blonde, thirtyish, with a thriving practice. Her specialty is problem pregnancies. Nanette went to her after two miscarriages.

Blocker was a thorough professional, the pregnancy a breeze. I know that's easy for me to say, but Nanette confirms it. Point is, we were taken with Dr. Blocker, imagined her private life to be as elegant and "with it" as her practice. The work would be hard and demanding, of course. Being a doctor is glamorous only from the patient's point of view. But Blocker was bound to be driving a champagne-colored Mercedes 450 SL home from the office. She had to be single with a flock of suitors, and we saw her weekends filled with tennis, horsey afternoons, and nights at Studebaker's and the Venetian Room.

Now, the big day had arrived, and there we were in delivery, Nanette supine, anesthetized from the waist down, while Dr. Blocker cut a bikini line below the navel and went in after Oren. The operation itself Nanette and I could not see, as a sheet had been strung between us and the surgical team. But we could hear the water break, and I could see blood spotting the floor beneath the table. The banter between Dr. Blocker and Dr. Hunt was light and full of fun, and occasionally, Nanette and I would join in. It was 8:30 in the morning, and the world could have been going to hell for all we knew. In that light, antiseptic room we were birthing the future. The conversation went something like this:

Dr. Blocker: Boy am I sore. My thighs and bottom are black and blue.

Dr. Hunt (surely raising his eyebrows behind his surgical mask): Dare we ask what you were up to?

Dr. Blocker (laughing): Horseback riding. I was taking riding lessons. These people were trying to teach me how to canter. I tried to keep my poise, but all I did was bounce and jiggle. The horse made a fool of me. My son got a kick out of it.

Nanette (from behind the sheet): You have children?

Dr. Blocker: Why, yes, punkin. I have a thirteen-year-old boy.

Nanette (a little high on happy gas): I can't imagine you having a kid that big. You're so young and beautiful. I just can't imagine.

Dr. Hunt: Here, here. She can't be more than thirty-seven.

Dr. Blocker: Want a kick under the table? Boy, Nanette, you have a strong stomach muscle.

Dr. Hunt: Here it comes. Here's the head.

Dr. Blocker: A dark head of hair.

Dr. Hunt: She's pretty enough to be a girl. Look at those long eyelashes.

Dr. Blocker: It is a girl!

Oren: Gurgle, gurgle.

Dr. Blocker: A lot of fluid.

Oren: Gurgle. Waaa. Waaa.

Nanette: Oh, God, we did it, Billy.

Billy: Hold me, hon. I may drop.

We were close about the car. The doc drives a sable Jaguar.

A LITTLE DANILOVA ON DIXIE CUPS

THIS IS AN AMERICAN FAIRY TALE that came true, as beautiful and inspiring a story as Grace Kelly's marriage to Rainier III, the prince of Monaco. So let's begin our tale the year Grace left Hollywood and went off to that Mediterranean castle.

It was 1953, and our hero, Art Dunham, was not doing as well as he had expected. Sure, he had married his hometown sweetheart, Bunnie Kuzma, the daughter of Woodbridge, New Jersey's Hungarian milkman, and the honeymoon was still on after three years. But Art himself was still knocking around in the minors, this at a time when the bloom on bush-league baseball was fading. In city after city, fans were abandoning the old clubs as the majors came to town. Art was still young, a left-handed pitcher-turned-outfielder. Baseball was still a white boy's game, and at six feet and 185 pounds, Art was a fair country slugger. As late as 1958, for the Dallas Rangers he hit .318 with 17 homers, 13 triples, and 39 doubles. But it had been ten years since the New York Giants had signed him after a tryout at the Polo Grounds. And he would never play there or at Chavez Ravine in Los Angeles.

Art ended his baseball career with the Dallas Rangers, retiring in 1959 at the age of 29. Became a traveling salesman, sold electrical supplies to utilities. Even more so than in baseball, he was still on the road, four days a week from January to December. But he and Bunnie felt more of a family now. They bought a little house, and Art made a point of starting his weekend on Friday, so he and Bunnie could have more time together. They wanted children worse than Bunnie had wanted to be a hoofer and Art had wanted to be a big leaguer. Mature now, they sought a life similar to the one their families had shared back in the old days in Woodbridge.

"We had a great growing up," Bunnie recalls. "Woodbridge had a small town feeling, but we were an hour by train from Manhattan. Arthur Dunham was a nice-looking boy, from an English/Pennsylvania

Dutch background. His dad was a local businessman. Art was a drummer, played in his own high school dance band, and I liked that. I had tap-danced until twelve, when my mother died. Art brought back the lilt in me and we had a good time. A typical date was to catch the train to Manhattan and head for the Paramount Theater, where Gene Krupa might be playing, or Tommy Dorsey or Benny Goodman. We'd have Chinese food and then catch the midnight train home…"

Art interrupts. "I believe in fate totally," he says, looking at me, and then looking to Bunnie to explain.

It is May 1987. We are in their comfortable ranch-style home on an Arcadian bluff that looks down on the lake, and, in the distant western horizon, the mirage of the big city's skyline. The homes in Rockwall where they live have huge yards, even pastures with barns and horses, and behind their yellow rail fence at 4 Shadydale Lane, the Dunhams have come to realize themselves in a very American way. Oh, Art is silver-haired and hefty now, and Bunnie is a doting grandmother. But they are far from retiring. Art is still on the road locally four days a week, drumming now (in the old sense) for Light Bulb Supply, Inc. Bunnie has been, for the past fifteen years, a teacher's aid at Rockwall Elementary Schools. They have a son, Jeffrey Charles, who, at 25, is employed at TU Electric Co. Like his father, six-foot-two Jeff is a gifted athlete. He enjoys playing slow-pitch softball on two successful teams and has been voted MVP by his teammates. He likes time with his wife, Donna, and their 18-month-old daughter, Jennifer. They live close by, and Jeff is as involved in his parents' lives as he ever was. Backyard family barbecues, weekends watching sports on television, sharing with the old man daily happenings in their lives.

The scene at the Dunhams' is right out of Norman Rockwell, even if the illustrator and the old *Saturday Evening Post* are long gone. But where's the fairy tale part, and what did Art mean by fate?

The fairy tale springs to life in Christine Dunham, their daughter, who, on that very night last May as we sat talking in Rockwall, was dancing a main role in the American Ballet Theater's production of *Giselle* at the Metropolitan Opera House in Manhattan. The next morning in *The New York Times*, critic Anna Kisselgoff wrote: "Christine Dunham, superb as Albrecht's disdainful fiancée, wears a spectacular red satin dress."

Within a month, Bunnie Kuzma Dunham would be back up at the clan house in Woodbridge, getting ready to catch the train to Manhattan to visit Christine and share in her biggest moment: signing her first soloist contract with the American Ballet Theater, which included an invitation to dance a five-minute pas de deux with Mikhail Baryshnikov in the July 6th filming of "Dance In America" in Denmark. This was the fate Art Dunham was talking about. It seems the old train trips to Manhattan to see the stars had paid off. The rattling ride between Woodbridge and Manhattan is as familiar to Bunnie and him—more, actually—than her sitting in half-empty grandstands watching him jog from the dugout to right field. And older than his rounds as a salesman. And newer, now, with Christine's name in lights. Art had hoped that his name would be up there, too, among the stars of America's national pastime. But for all his talent, for all his slavish dedication, fate, the breaks—whatever you call it—denied him his elevation. It was as if the gods had said, "We can't take you, but we will your daughter." And he had accepted it, believing it had been fixed from the beginning. All those long train trips had not been for nothing. It was all preparation for the apprenticeship and grooming of a gifted young dancer he and Bunnie were destined to deliver to the world. A ballerina blooming forth from an old baseball slugger? Why not? Behind the French terminology and the prima donna pose, the same limbs were at work to make the most marvelous move seem commonplace. It was damn hard work. Practice, practice, practice, whether on the barre or at the plate. Christina was, after all, a chip off the old block.

And to think that once they thought she would never be born.

"We'd been married for eight years," Art recalls, "and were thinking of going to Hope Cottage to adopt a baby, when Christine was conceived."

Christine Ellen Dunham was born November 3, 1958, in the Chester Clinic. Dr. Douglas Hardy delivered her. She was brought home to the house in Casa View. When Christine was ten, the Dunhams moved across the new lake, high on the grassy Eden of Rockwall—where the fairy tale would begin, but very quietly, and with such labor and determination it was a wonder the budding ballerina had a childhood.

"She was always musical," Bunnie says. "Art still plays the bongos, and that's how Christine started dancing, to his beat. And as a daughter, she still dances to his tempo. Art is an old-fashioned father. He makes the decisions, even when he's in a motel on the road. Christine is her own woman now, an accomplished artist, but she still gets on the phone and talks things over with Dad. He handles the big picture, and I tend to the details.

"Now, of course, ballet was not one of Art's passions, so the hoofer part must have come from me. One day we looked up and Christine had stuck her toes in Dixie cups and was on point, tip-toeing across the floor like Danilova in toe shoes."

Miss Joy, who still teaches dance, looked at the six-year-old Christine and said to Mrs. Dunham, "Your baby has the perfect body for ballet."

Christine was a serious student from the start, so Bunnie enrolled her in the ambitious Cranford House studio in Lochwood Village. Lorraine and Don Cranford told Mrs. Dunham, "You've got a winner." Eventually, Myrtha Rosello, a Cuban Bay of Pigs refugee, and her husband, Carlos, took over the Cranford House and, under their tutelage, Christine bloomed. Ms. Rosello had been a professional dancer under the famous ballerina Alicia Alonzo, and she was demanding.

So was the schedule for this exceptional child. It was twenty-one miles by car from Rockwall to the Cranford House. Then twenty-one miles back. Bunnie would pick her up after school and drive to the studio while Christine changed into leotards and ate a snack. She would work out at the studio while Bunnie watched. They would get home at eight, after a fourteen-hour day.

The Dunhams did not push Christine. In fact, they worried about her overdoing things. She did everything to the best of her ability, and she was prodigious in her interest. Dance was important, but so was her little brother, her cats and dogs and horses, and, eventually, her schoolmates and boyfriends. During her last years of high school in Rockwall, Christine insisted on being a cheerleader and drill team member, which required her to return to school after ballet class.

By this time, Christine was driving herself to the Metropolitan Ballet Co., where she now trained in classes every evening. Art recalls: "We always worried about her making it through the mixmaster on the Interstate, so around eight, when she was due to hit it, we'd jump in my car and meet her at the mixmaster. She was sixteen and driving what we called the Brown Bomber, an old Ford Maverick. She'd toot her horn and wave, and we would turn around and follow her to make sure she got home safely, this kid in black leotards and a pink tutu."

At ten, Christine had as her first dance partner a dark-haired boy named Graydon Vandament. At twelve, she won her first scholarship to the School of American Ballet at Lincoln Center, the prep school for George Balanchine's New York City Ballet. Christine was not alone. Four other dancers from Ms. Rosello's class were called as well: the Vandament boy, Kim Hoffman, Carol Aschim, and Shenikwa Nolan. In the next six years Christine would win six more scholarships at Lincoln Center. The school was for six weeks in June and July, and the first two years Bunnie went with Christine. They stayed at the Kuzma home in Woodbridge, and commuted to Manhattan.

"After each summer session, Mrs. Dunham recalls, "Christine was invited to stay fulltime because she was certainly a promising young prospect. But socially and mentally, she would have died on the vine. She was a sweet young lady, a Texas hothouse flower, and New York City was scary." Within three years, though, Christine was allowed to stay on her own at a hotel for young ladies near Lincoln Center. Her favorite teachers at the academy included Alexandra Danilova, Andre Kramarevsky, and Stanley Williams.

By 1978, Christine was confident enough to join the new Dallas Ballet, and in a troupe of strong young dancers she stood out. In September of 1979, I first saw Miss Dunham dance under the stars at Lee Park. I wrote in the Dallas Times Herald: "There was a point, however, in *Don Quixote*, when I thought the control tower choreography from Love Field was going to drown out Minkus and screw up Skibine, but Christine Dunham and Allan Kinzie held to it beautifully…" I went on to say that I whistled under my breath at the precision and beauty of Christine's dancing. The company's artistic director, George Skibine, became a second father to Christine, and he led her on a steady, sure course, careful not to push too hard too fast. The result was that she remained with the local ballet for seven years, the last five under the old Danish wizard Fleming Flindt.

She had chances to fly on to bigger things, but Christine herself did not feel the moment was right, even when others were applauding. In May, 1980, columnist John Branch announced that Christine was one of eight American dancers invited to compete in the International Ballet Competition in Varna, Bulgaria, that July. Branch observed: "Ms. Dunham and her American teammates will be competing for medals that have been won by Mikhail Baryshnikov, Fernando Bujones, Yoko Morishita, and Suzanne Longley.

"So it's quite a step into prominence that Ms. Dunham is taking. There's no way of comparing her with the other members of the American team (beyond noting that the scoring used in the selection process ranked her second), but locally she is certainly in the top rank."

Her third year with the Dallas Ballet, Christine married Michael Zembower, a Baltimore native and aspiring actor, and thereafter she danced as Christine Zembower. It was through Ms. Rosello's connections that in 1985 Christine got an audition with Fernando Bujones, principal with American Ballet Theater, and it was because of Bujones' recommendation that Baryshnikov himself auditioned her that summer. When she finished, he called her over.

"Christine," he said, "you are a soloist, and we have no room in our company except in the corps."

"Then I'll go in the corps," she said without a blink.

She called home to the antique brick house on the bluff in Rockwall and informed her parents of her decision. She said, "Mom, Dad, I want to try New York."

Art said, "Honey, you may wake up at forty and say, 'Why didn't I do that?' Go for it!"

Christine and Michael moved to Manhattan and got an apartment a block off Broadway and Lincoln Center so they could walk to the theater. It was expensive, but between them they made it. While in search of solid acting roles, Mike made money working at Columbus, a popular New York restaurant, while Christine danced in the great company's corps. She decided to dance again in her own name, for professional reasons, but it was two years before Anna Kisselgoff of the *New York Times* noticed her in print. At last, on April 20, 1987, she wrote a review of "Sleeping Beauty": "The women dance in short tutus generally against scenery that comes from the same palette. There are several exceptions. One is Christine Dunham, in violet and enormously impressive in the standard Lilac Fairy variation."

Then, only weeks later, the soloist contract and the big invitation from Baryshnikov.

Art Dunham called me on the phone. "This is one of the greatest days of our lives," the old slugger said. "Bunnie will be home shortly and we'll get together."

I recalled something Mrs. Dunham had said that first time I asked how it was between her husband

and her daughter.

"It's very special," she said. "Such deep respect on both sides. They talk deep talk. But Christine is proud and he never pushed or bullied. I left when they settled into one another, but I sensed Art's way. He said things in a certain way so that she understood cause and effect, and she grew up a good kid. Ballet helped. It is so demanding."

On Christine's mature character, her father says: "Christy is a loner, sort of. She'd have to be to have achieved what she has, and she's just begun, if you can believe that, after all these years. She's sociable but careful and particular, as graceful as her dancing. Like Bunnie says, quite the young lady and very professional, but tough and thrives on competition. But at home she's a shirt-tail gal, eats barbecued chicken, baked potatoes and cornbread, longs to ride the horses again. The Zembowers are just moments away too, and we have a fine family time. Christy is very protective of her animals, which we keep, and they include a dog, Chi-Chi, bitch of a pasture dog named Tramp. The unusual thing about Chi-Chi is that she is eighteen years old, has never been to a vet, except for shots, and is only a little slow. Then there's the cats, Turbo, Duffy, and Topsy."

Bunnie says of the first 21 years of ballet, "I tied the bows, wiped her tears away, and Art went to her performances and enjoyed them, some would say in the oddest way."

"How's that?"

"Well," he explained, rather sheepishly, "If I think things are going right, I cry all the time. I sit there among a thousand people with tears streaming down my face. Then, I'll catch myself. Maybe I'm crying for the wrong reason, maybe Christy's not doing so well. What do I know about ballet? Baseball? Lemme tell ya. But ballet? So I look to Bunnie, and she lets me know if I'm right. And if it is right we both cry."

SCRAM

THE ORGANIST HAD STARTED to play the wedding march, but Gary knew when he walked into the dressing room to take Sheila's satiny arm in his that something was wrong. He could see it in her tight, pouty, little face. They were now alone.

"Hey, baby, are we all right?"

"Sure," she said, a crack in her voice.

He took a big hand and turned her face up into his. A tear rolled from her lashes and dropped into his palm.

"Tell Daddy the truth. Do you still love Harry?"

"I hate him," she confessed, not avoiding her father's eyes.

"Why do this then?"

"It's too late, you know that, Daddy. I can't let you and Mom and Harry's folks down. The church is full of everyone I've ever known in my life…"

"None of that makes a bit of difference. Baby, my Corvette is waiting outside. We can make a dash for it now. Just you and me. Let's scram. Leave Mom to work it out with Harry and his and all the rest. We'll blow to Mexico, go to Disneyland, do anything you want until things quiet down. We don't have to come back until you're ready. And then we'll come back high, wide, and handsome. How 'bout it?"

"Daddy, she's playing the march over again. Come on, we're late. Let's go through with it."

They left the room, marched into the foyer, and then came down the aisle as all heads turned toward them.

Gary kept his head high and his teeth on display, but through them he kept muttering, "Don't take another step toward that creep at the altar. Let's turn and make a break for it. Let's scram."

She pretended not to hear.

But halfway down the aisle, she stopped, looked up beseechingly at her father, and said, "Daddy, take me away, quickly, or I'll faint."

Gary kept his arm-lock on her. They turned around and marched toward the door. A murmur went through the congregation. At the altar, Harry, Jr., and Harry, Sr., who was best man, almost broke their necks turning back and forth in bewilderment. For now Gary and Sheila were running, flying through the door, into the foyer and out the main door. They went down the steps and fell into the red Corvette. The engine fired and roared and away they went.

Gretchen did not see them for four days. But, of course, they talked by phone before Gary and Sheila started for Disneyland.

How had she felt, being left to deal with...?

"I was never so relieved in my life as when I saw them run out of that church," she said. "I turned to the Harrys, told them I was sorry the gods had dumped on us, but that perhaps it was for the best. They and their crowd went off in a huff. My friends and I, well, we went to the country club and ate and drank and partied into the night. It was the best time I've had since my honeymoon."

No Baby Talk

BEFORE THE BABY CAME, my wife spent hours decorating the nursery, a small bedroom on the northeast side of the house. Since I had had children in another life, I felt qualified to step in and set her straight lest she get off on the wrong foot. Right away, I was firm and to the point.

"The baby will be much better off if we keep the Disneyesque characters out of its room," I said. "Let's stay away from pinks and blues and yellows, and, please, no decals of cute little animals stuck to every stick of furniture. I suggest a classic white theme throughout, with an occasional toy or touch of color to tempt the eye. But keep the accessories restrained and to a minimum. The kid's mind will be trashed soon enough without our help, but at least we can start it off right."

"Aren't you being a little severe?" Nanette said. "The kid is not going to come out of the womb with a PhD in aesthetics and logic. What's wrong with slurpy fantasy and a few sickeningly sweet childish metaphors?

"They tend to stick throughout life, that's what," I said. "And they are hardly the adequate symbols and references this baby will need to face the future. Do you realize the child will be twenty-one in 2005?"

"Are you sure you want this baby?" Nanette said, looking anxiously at her swollen stomach.

"Why, of course," I said. "How could you ask such a thing?"

"I don't know. You sound awfully negative. Sometimes I think you'd rather have a child prodigy than a cuddly little baby."

"See!" I said. "You're already doing the thing that I really do dread."

"And that is . . ."

"You're equating having a baby with all those infantile, sentimental totems that commonplace little minds have conjured up. It is a cartoon way of looking at an infant, so silly and simpy that I can't believe you would fall for it. You must not be the intellect I married. God, I'll look up one day and hear you talking baby talk to the child."

It was a nasty dig, and unfair. Her dark eyes clouded and her lower lip quivered, but she bore up and went ahead with the baby's room. Figuring I had more than made my point, I stepped back and let her see it through alone. She closed the doors and worked in secret, scraping, painting, hauling furnishings in from family and layaway.

And the day she opened it for me to see I was quite pleased. The walls were off-white, the curtains bleached muslin, the crib an old-fashioned spool bed painted icebox white. She had taken my grandfather's small, dark armoire and covered it with a high gloss white. The only color in the room was the old iron double bed, which she had sprayed tractor red. It was covered with a red-and-white patterned quilt my Aunt Marguerite had made. Seeing not one anthropomorphic animal or idealized babe, I pronounced my approval.

It was then that she said, "Look up."

Around the border of the wall and ceiling marched a procession of bright blue half-moons and red stars, which she tediously had stenciled and painted. I stared at them as a child would from its crib, and smiled. "It works," I had to admit.

The room you would not recognize now, and the baby's only been home three months. The clean white that dominated the nursery has been overwhelmed by an array of colorful characters, contraptions, and toys, some dating back to my own childhood. Well, I couldn't resist when my sister brought them out of mothballs. Then I had to give Nanette permission to include hers. One has to believe in continuity. Friends and family did the rest. My favorites are the mobile carousel that plays "Brahms Lullaby," the yellow windup lamb that, of course, plays "Mary Had a Little Lamb," and the woolly bear named Liza Doolittle that growls so charmingly when you lay her down to sleepy-pooh.

I spend delicious time in the nursery, rocking Snookums and smelling her yum-yum-yummy neck.

DON JOHNSON HIMSELF

While we criticize the fathers for being narrow, we should not forget
that they were also deep. We are inclined to be so broad that people
can see through us most any place.

—from a sermon by William Hiram Foulkes

FOR EIGHTY YEARS, he's lived in the same shady spot across the road from the general store in
Miller Grove. And during all that time, no one has ever had anything untoward to report about Don
Johnson.

At least not until the other day. But let's not get ahead of the story.

What can you say about a man who, in 1927, won the hand of Miss Edna, the new first-grade teacher
in Miller Grove. What but good can you say about a man who doesn't cuss or tell off-color stories, who
for years paid the light bill at the Methodist Church and who, when the shriveling congregation
considered calling it quits, got up and said, "Well, I can tell you this. Regardless of what you decide, I
intend for there to be a church to bring up my children in, and that's that." What can you say about a
farmer/house painter whose three kids earned doctorates? Patsy Johnson Hallman is an author and
professor of home economics at Stephen F. Austin State University. Lynn Johnson is professor of
business at North Texas State. And Coy Johnson became a lawyer in Sulphur Springs, the county seat,
where he is a wealthy and powerful figure.

The worst you can say about Don Johnson is that he is a man of few words, has a habit of cutting off
the conversation after he's had his say, especially when he's talking on the telephone. As a friend put it,

"Don has a low toleration for gibble-gabble."

Case in point: Mollie McKool was taking pictures of Don and his daughter Patsy for this book. Don sat as still as the stones that lie at the base of the great oak under which he abides.

"Mr. Johnson, please talk or say something," Mollie pleaded from behind her various cameras lined up on stands, pointing at Mr. Johnson like a firing squad. "Patsy, engage him in conversation."

"Daddy," Patsy said. "Tell us about why the church had to be picked up and turned around to face the opposite direction."

"Because they moved the road behind it," Mr. Johnson said.

That was all Patsy could get out of him.

We mentioned the tree. Except on the coldest days, you can usually find him sitting under the three-hundred-year-old live oak beside his house, a small, erect man with white hair and blue eyes, his back against the west wind—except at sunset, when he'll shift to watch the colors on the horizon. Lou, the beautiful lady he married after Miss Edna's death, says Little Don, as she calls him, would sleep out there into the night if she didn't call him in at bedtime. The oak may be Johnson's oldest friend. His children say it was a big tree when Don first played under it and in it as a four-year-old in 1906.

But the man doesn't gather moss. If Johnson isn't under his tree, you're likely to find him fishing in a neighborhood pond or tooling around country roads in his car, which he is careful to keep within the bounds of Hopkins County. Daughter Patsy says for some reason Don thinks it unsafe to get beyond the county line. He may be right.

But his passion is gardening. For years Johnson has kept the largest plot in Miller Grove. He is in his rows from New Year's until November, and his onions and yams, peas and okra are bounty for friends' tables.

Which brings us to Snip, a paint plowhorse that has tramped and pulled ahead of Don Johnson for so long people think of them as inseparable. To ponder the age of Snip and the time of his service to his master is to wonder when the first perch in Turkey Creek ate the first minnow.

Small wonder that the other day Don Johnson took a hard look at Snip, decided it was time to retire him and get a new plowhorse. "Just as well get some money for him," he said, and advertised Snip for sale in the county paper.

A man from Sulphur Springs phoned about Snip, and Lou talked to him. He turned out to be Frank Odom, a deacon in the Baptist church where Lou used to teach Sunday school. Odom said he needed a gentle horse for his kids, and Lou said Snip was the gentlest thing, which he is. She also said she knew Snip to be over ten years old, which is the truth. Fact of the matter, he was probably that fifteen years ago.

Anyway, Deacon Odom came out to Miller Grove. Don put a bridle on Snip and led him to the porch. The debate at the general store across the street now centers around the business of the bridle. If it had been a harness, it probably would have been all right. Snip's used to wearing a harness. But a bridle? How long has it been since Don got up on his back? No telling.

We can tell you that Deacon Odom did not stay long on Snip's back. As soon as he crawled on, Snip started bucking.

Don was flabbergasted. "I've never seen him do that," he swore to Deacon Odom. So help him, it was the truth. And who's to question a man like Don Johnson? Deacon Odom tried a second time, got the same welcome. The red-faced gentleman retrieved his hat, dusted it off, put it on, and retreated to Sulphur Springs. Sans Snip, of course.

It's a good man that can't get rid of a gentle horse. Old Snip knows a good home when he's got one.

I say the other day, but that was in December of '84. Time doesn't mean a lot out here. Anyway, the following spring, Don Johnson came down with a fever that had not only Lou worried, but the whole village.

Right off, folks knew something wasn't right. You see, at least a dozen things have to happen daily in Miller Grove for people to know that life is going on as usual, and Mr. Johnson is in charge of five of them. Well, six if you count Sundays. Buck Woodard and Curt Ethridge are responsible for five. And the Waskoms have to open the store.

Mr. Woodard, a retired farmer who is almost blind but can drive pretty good to the store and to church, has to show up at Waskom's General Store and sit on the porch. Then, at some point around noon, he is expected to get up and go inside and get a pint of milk, which he takes back out on the porch to savor. He is a nice man to talk to, and it's a cattywampus day, indeed, when he isn't pleasant and sharing of himself.

Mr. Ethridge, a farmer, hunter and general handyman, has to show up at the store too, but he usually hangs around inside being friendly unless he's needed outside in a neighborly way.

Don Johnson is not as outgoing, but there is such dignity and steadfastness in him that people count on him as well to keep the demeanor of the village even and ongoing. He has to sit under his oak, work his garden, give away most of its goodies,, go fishing or driving around the county, and keep the Methodist Church going. Once in a while, he'll get up and go chat with Buck or Curt at the store, but people don't count on it the way they do other things. If you're keeping count, you know we've still got one more thing to go before things are dandy in Miller Grove. It is this: the domino game in the shack behind the store. It must go on, as it has for generations.

Well, you can imagine everyone's concern that June when the Waskoms opened the store, Buck did his part, Curt his, the domino players theirs, but Don Johnson was nowhere to be seen. The fact that it was darn near 100 degrees outside made no difference. Heat had never stopped Mr. Johnson.

This time it had, his own heat, that is. Mr. Johnson's prostate got to acting up, and the infection sent his temperature soaring. Lou put him to bed and called his kids, who found him so weak and dehydrated he could hardly move. They took turns nursing him.

The day that daughter Patsy was there, Mr. Johnson got to feeling better and wanted to go out and sit under the oak. Patsy and Lou helped him to his swing under a low, massive limb. After a while, Mr. Johnson got up and decided he was going to walk across 275 to Waskom's Store. Patsy rushed out to help him. He was weak, hardly able to stand, she says.

"No, I can manage myself," Mr. Johnson said to his daughter and she could tell from his tone that he would rather fall than have to lean on a woman out there on the public road. So Patsy backed into the house and watched through a window as he made his way.

Clearly, it was a terrible effort for Mr. Johnson. He moved slowly, ever so tediously, wobbling on his still painful joints, and Patsy thought of the story of the snail:

"A snail was crossing the road for seven years. Just as he got across, a tree fell and barely missed him by an inch or two. If he had been where he was six months before, it would've killed him. The snail looked at the tree and told people, 'See, it pays to be fast.'"

Patsy looked at the great oak which had stood so long. She looked at her father who had stood so long. She could not wait seven years to learn if her father was or wasn't going to be flattened on the asphalt. She picked up the phone and called Waskom's.

"Pam," she said, "Daddy's trying to cross the road to come to the store, and you know how sick he's been. Can you have James come out and help him?"

Patsy hadn't put the receiver down when she saw James Waskom break from the store like Secretariat from the starting gate, his strong, strawberry-roan figure striding confidently, breaking down the distance between him and the wispy but dignified figure that was her father. James stopped before Mr. Johnson, offered his hand in greeting, and a manful understanding passed between them, the specifics of which Patsy could only suppose.

She watched as James extended a ruddy Herculean arm, and she saw through clouded eyes her father take the arm of the younger man, nod matter-of-factly, and begin again his journey across the road and into the store.

It was only a few days before Don Johnson was himself again, and things seemed back to normal in Miller Grove. Buck was at his post, Curt at his, the Waskoms at theirs, the domino players in the back in the shack.

But we were wrong when we said time doesn't matter in Miller Grove. Time finally nipped old Snip, and Don Johnson was bereft for days. Then Buck Woodard had a stroke that keeps him bound to his house. The Waskoms up and sold the store to their cousins, Johnny and Gail Darrow, and moved away, clear out of the country.

Curt's still hanging in there, though, and so is Don Johnson. He has a man with a young plowhorse to turn up his furrows now, and as Mollie took pictures of him and Patsy last summer, he insisted everyone take home a sack of red onions.

Of her father and his tree, Patsy writes:

My strongest recollection of total peace is a cool May afternoon with my mother and father sitting together in a porch swing which hung in the tree branches. They talked quietly as I got up to play nearby with my brothers and friends. Under the big tree I've swung in the child's swing as high as my courage would allow; I've played dolls for hours on end; have shared adolescent girl-talk with cousins; have sat with boyfriends and lovers, husbands; read for hours book after book under the oak; and as a girl and woman shelled many a pea and cut corn for canning and freezing. In that shade I've had endless conversations with my brothers and their families, have hosted friends from near and far. And it was under that tree that we gathered on a hot August afternoon in 1975 after burying Mother. Somehow, it has always drawn us, is the fitting place to be.

It's one of God's finest creations, and it is where we go to see Daddy, the noble old man who still lives in its shade.

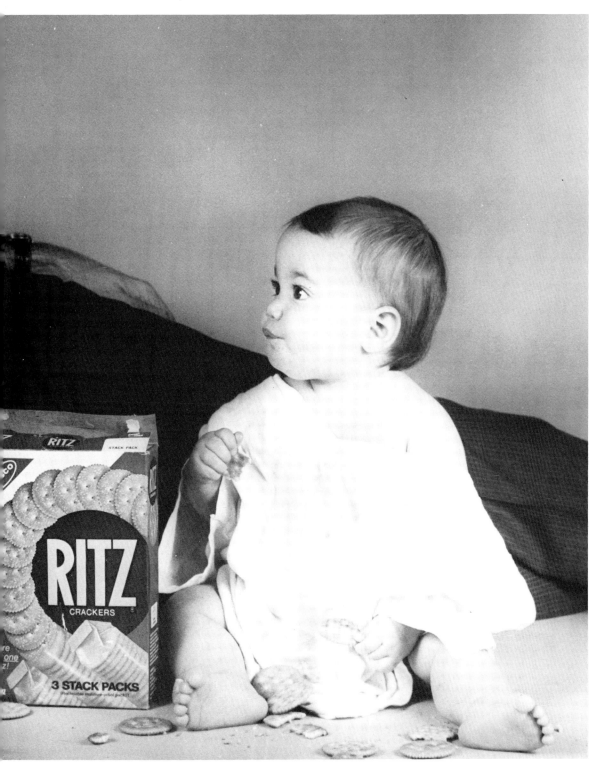

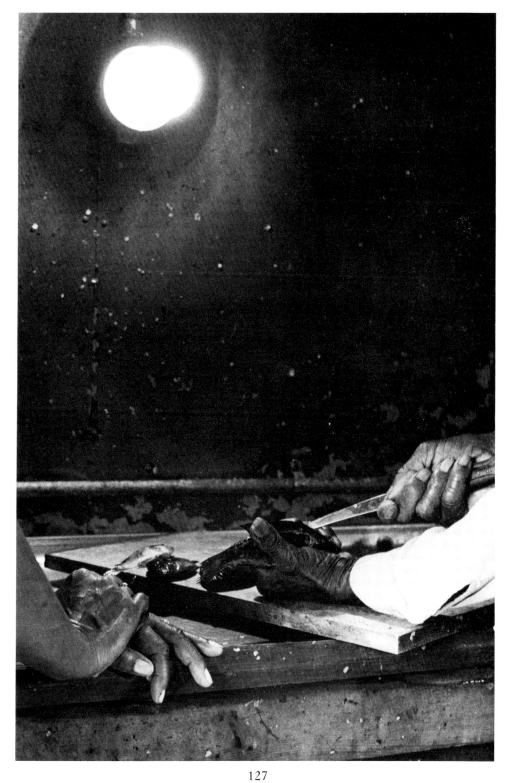

WONDERFUL AND APPALLING

Late middle-age is no time for rest, with decrepitude and the slow slide to oblivion around the corner. So I work as hard as when I was young and ambitious, except now my storing up of nuts takes less of my whole existence, being practiced and skilled, and I look up often and take in more of the world around me, circumscribed as it is on my little farm. And what I see are daughters, not all of my girls, but the two who still circle about—the fair Erin now a woman heavy with child, the dark Oren already three and flashing long lashes and her mother's undeniable will. Thank God for these two. Old Dinah Craik was right when she wrote:

> *Oh, my son's a son till he gets him a wife,*
> *But my daughter's my daughter all her life.*

Even King Lear could say that of Cordelia, if not the other two. How wretched he was till Cordelia proved true, and how painfully and equally have I repeated his grief. And doubled his joy. Then am I richer than he? Are two faithful daughters better than one? It's silly to compare, isn't it? Each to his own.

Numbers are alien to me anyway, though I have built them up and knocked them down in years and wives. Like Solomon, I would take one true wife for all the rest. But this is age speaking, and all too self-righteously. Still, the gray beard has its advantages. I see and receive my children more fully than the clean-shaven father I was at thirty-four, have even learned to let my son Winton go and come at his will, not mine. The same with Erin. Oren wants the freedom already and gets Lebanese-mad when, like an old collie, I herd her away from the rattlesnake grass. Although she and her half-sister are moon and sun, Oren will, in her blooming, be as much to handle as Erin was. The combination of Celt and Arab is compelling if volatile, as her mother and I learned. But I welcome the day and even the difficulty because it would mean that I lived long enough to see her flower. I wonder if I might see her through the rough spots, see her all the way through the rye? But no, that's asking too much. One would have to live forever. My father died two summers ago at the age of eighty-five, still thinking his sons were crazy, and he had a point. He made our younger sister the executrix of the estate, and she has meant the difference between war and peace.

Erin carried on my romantic foolhardiness in her youth, but these days, nearing thirty and settled with her man, carrying his child, she is suddenly, it seems, mature and sensible, adroit at soothing tempers, much like her aunt, my sister Joyce. Where once Erin created chaos, now she brings order and understanding. She hasn't become a simp to others. She still belongs to herself, but she doesn't beat her breast about it the way she did. We've always had a thing, even as I dictated and she rebelled, and often I find her taking care of me, in a teasing, gentle way, as if I am the child and she the parent. It is rich, our being equals, so bound in blood and spirit. And the richest time of all is when the four of us—Billy, Erin, Winton and Oren—are together on the farm, pitching horseshoes and laughing until dusk. By the time you read this, there will be a fifth, my first grandchild, and she will be Bailey or he will be Addison, unless Erin and Ed change their minds, which they probably will.

The future is in our children, but there's no telling what they'll do with it, save to suppose the same thing we did. It is both wonderful and appalling to consider.

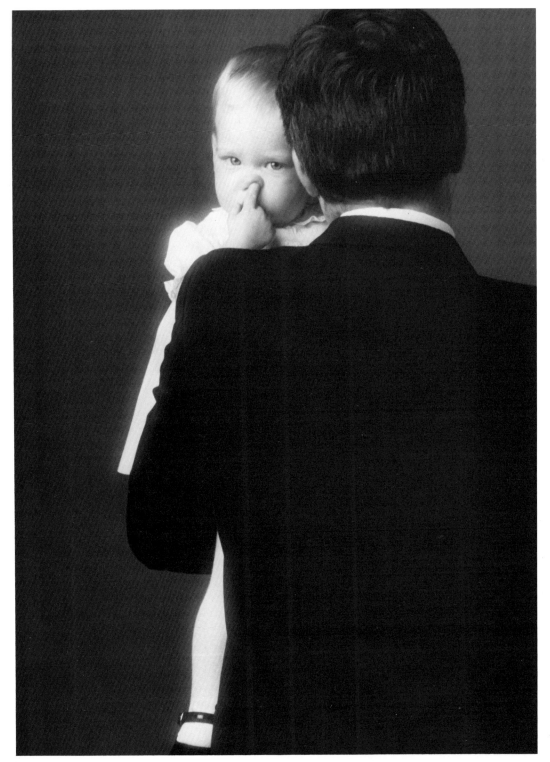